COLLEGE FOR THE COMMONWEALTH

COLLEGE
FOR THE
COMMONWEALTH

A Case for Higher Education in American Democracy

Michael T. Benson and Hal R. Boyd

Foreword by E. Gordon Gee

 UNIVERSITY PRESS OF KENTUCKY

Editorial and Sales Offices: The University Press of Kentucky
663 South Limestone Street, Lexington, Kentucky 40508-4008
www.kentuckypress.com

Cataloging-in-Publication data is available from the Library of Congress.

ISBN 978-0-8131-7659-8 (hardcover : alk. paper)
ISBN 978-0-8131-7660-4 (epub)
ISBN 978-0-8131-7661-1 (pdf)

This book is printed on acid-free paper meeting
the requirements of the American National Standard
for Permanence in Paper for Printed Library Materials.

Manufactured in the United States of America.

Member of the Association of University Presses

Contents

Foreword

During my career, I have been fortunate to serve as president of five universities: Brown, Colorado, Ohio State, Vanderbilt, and West Virginia. Each institution in its own way has helped me to see and understand the extraordinary impact of higher education. It is one of my greatest joys as president to share the message about the importance and value of higher education with anyone, from students and parents to reporters and legislators.

This message has a special resonance when I am talking about the role of higher education in strengthening our democracy. This is a fundamental but often overlooked point. By preparing educated citizens, taxpayers, and voters who will think critically, ask tough questions, and assert their opinions, our universities and colleges are continually hitting the "refresh" button on America's civic web page. Our democracy is much stronger and more vibrant as a result. Michael Benson and Hal Boyd put this point front and center in their book, and all of us who are champions for the value of higher education have a powerful new tool for framing this essential message.

It is no accident that Benson and Boyd employ the word "Commonwealth" in the title of their book. In their capable hands, the word does double duty: the authors remind us of the enormously positive impact that higher education has had on America's shared democracy and prosperity, and simultaneously they make a compelling case for reinvestment in higher education by Kentucky's state government. The authors are very eloquent on both counts. Higher education does, indeed, contribute substantially to our "common wealth" in each of our states and across all of our society.

Let me offer an example featuring two places I know well, West Virginia and Ohio. A few years ago, West Virginia University and The Ohio State University joined forces to launch the Marcellus Shale Energy and Environmental Laboratory to make the most of the natural gas that lay under these two states. We brought industry (Northeast Natural Energy) and a national laboratory (the National Energy Technology Laboratory) to the table as partners for the first comprehensive, long-term field study of shale gas resources. This multifaceted partnership conducts research and generates knowledge that will help to guide the transformation of our states' respective economies—and our nation's energy usage mix. (The partnership also gives a whole new meaning to the old expression, "Now you're cooking with gas.")

To make their case about the value of American higher education, Benson and Boyd employ a skillfully syncretic blend of voices, from Aristotle and Aesop to Wendell Berry and J. D. Vance, to illuminate the challenges that confront higher education. While you may have read some of these authors before, I predict that you will see their words in a different light after reading how Benson and Boyd apply them in this context. If you are looking for new arrows for your rhetorical quiver in defense of higher education, you will find them in these pages.

The authors also offer an effectively eclectic set of examples to illustrate potential solutions for higher education. From continuous improvement in Toyota's automobile plants to self-correction and accountability in child welfare offices in Alabama and Utah, Benson and Boyd demonstrate how higher education can learn from other domains. Gathering together these anecdotes from disparate sources is another strength of this volume. The authors' astute analysis of how these approaches can improve higher education is significant value added.

I appreciate that Benson and Boyd do not, as some critics of higher education have done, simply point to success in other sectors of our society and economy as perfect exemplars and chastise higher education for not blindly following that lead. Academe is different from business and government. That seems like common sense, but common sense is not a flower that grows in everyone's garden. Lessons are transferable from one sector to another, but the transfer requires thought and creativity. This book serves as a useful how-to guide.

I also applaud Benson and Boyd's unapologetic conviction that each state has something to teach all of the others. As US Supreme Court justice Louis Brandeis observed, "A single courageous state may, if their citizens so choose, serve as a laboratory and try novel social and economic experiments without risk to the rest of the country." I believe Benson and Boyd are calling on Kentucky to be such a courageous state, and I believe the Bluegrass State will benefit if it heeds their call. I believe there is wisdom to be gleaned from the experience and experimentation of smaller, more rural states such as Kentucky—and my own state of West Virginia. We may not always get it right, but then again, the best ideas do not invariably come from the coasts or the largest cities. The places that make up "flyover country" have something to contribute, and this book captures that spirit admirably.

There is no shortage of books about higher education. There may be, however, a shortage of concise, insightful, relevant, and useful books about higher education. Benson and Boyd's fine work goes a long way toward filling that gap. Thanks to them, now whenever I think and talk about the importance and value of public higher education to American democracy, I will have an excellent resource on which to rely.

E. Gordon Gee
Morgantown, West Virginia

Introduction

Making the Case for Reinvestment

When he encountered Kentucky's frontier for the first time, folk hero Daniel Boone christened the land "a second paradise." He returned to his family "with a determination to bring them as soon as possible."[1] Today, the Commonwealth still boasts lush landscapes and natural resources; yet, as the globally competitive economy is increasingly knowledge based, Kentucky's fertile minds are as important as the state's fertile soil.[2] The Daniel Boones of tomorrow will be as attracted to the state's human resources as the natural ones.

While the race to educate an innovative workforce surges, Kentucky is sustaining some of the nation's largest per-student cuts to higher education.[3] In spring 2016, Kentucky's governor mandated that public colleges and universities carve out 4.5 percent from their midyear appropriations (it was eventually reduced to 2 percent). The governor also proposed eliminating 9 percent of state funding for the 2017–2018 biennium (the legislature reduced it to 4.5 percent). What's more, by 2020, state appropriations will be subject to performance metrics for all state-funded institutions.[4] And, according to Kentucky state budget director John Chilton, in order "to be fiscally responsible," the state will need to free up an additional "$1 billion per year" to address the pension shortfall. As a result, according to the *Courier-Journal,* universities are "sure to take another big whack."[5] In response to the governor's end-of-year press conference warning that the upcoming $20 billion biannual budget would "not be pretty," chair of the House Education Committee John "Bam" Carney ominously warned: "Higher education, I'm afraid, will probably see some drastic cuts."[6]

In short, public higher education in Kentucky could receive nearly $200 million less in 2018 than it did in 2008 (a 30 percent reduction).[7] In the governor's defense, the most recent cuts are the consequence of a vastly underfunded state pension system not of his creation. But this posture toward higher education did not begin with pensions, and it is by no means endemic to Kentucky. According to data from the Center on Budget and Policy Priorities, America's states today spend an average 20 percent less per student than seven years ago.[8] Although new reports show a gradual uptick in state funds as the economy stabilizes, the history of cuts over the past decade has resulted in continued tuition hikes and large per-student loan debt.[9]

Kentucky's governor chose to exempt several state agencies from the chopping block, but higher education was not one of them. As the state announced a new policy of austerity toward higher education, it also outlined the agencies and initiatives that it would continue to fund.[10] All of them are commendable: they include increased pay for police officers and other public safety personnel, reduction in caseloads for social workers, additional resources for prosecutors, and no cuts to Medicaid. The state chose, understandably, to protect some of the most vulnerable in our population. One critique of this approach is that, without funding higher education, the state is treating symptoms of societal ills while it neglects the underlying malaise. Education, especially higher education, is a medicine that targets root causes. In the triage of treatment, it must remain paramount.

We make the case here that education, and higher education in particular, remains vital for the Commonwealth. Even with the rising cost of tuition, a college degree is still a very sound personal financial investment. More than that, however, we make the case that universities enhance society; through increased knowledge, innovation, and economic development, universities act as catalysts to promote a healthier, civically minded, law-abiding populace that sustains stable democratic systems both locally and abroad.

This book is designed for policy makers and general audiences who seek to understand the continuing contributions of higher education within America's twenty-first-century republic to support civic virtues and to help create an environment in which the Commonwealth can flourish. We draw on data, but also on historical narratives, philosophy, social science, and anecdotes, to demonstrate the continuing need to invest in one of America's most successful institutions at promoting social mobility, economic growth, social innovation, and sound governance.

Our book comes at a critical time as higher education's value, direction, and relevancy are commonly called into question. Brandon Busteed, executive director of Education and Workforce Development at Gallup, reported that the Grand Old Party (GOP) had "soured" on higher education. The majority of Republican attitudes in recent years went from positive to negative regarding academe. That this dramatic reversal of opinion has happened since 2015 is even more alarming.[11] A recent Gallup survey revealed that 67 percent of members of the GOP have "very little confidence," or just "some" confidence, in colleges and universities.[12] A 2017 Pew Research Center survey found that 58 percent of Republicans responded that the university's effect on the direction of the country is negative.[13] The change is significant, especially considering Pew's

2015 survey in which, Busteed reports, 37 percent said it was negative and 54 percent positive. Busteed concludes:

> Republicans' souring on higher education has happened in just the past two years. These events and trends have triggered a significant amount of news coverage, particularly in—but hardly limited to—conservative media: student protests over race relations and inequality, the ways in which campuses handled these protests, debates over free speech, and the blocking of controversial (and primarily conservative) speakers. The events, trends and coverage have heightened the perception that colleges and universities are "too liberal." The implications of this collective conclusion are potentially devastating for higher education. The fallout could include fewer students (especially conservatives and children of conservative parents) enrolling in postsecondary education, students selecting institutions that are aligned with their political beliefs, reduced funding for higher education in conservative states, and more contentious debates about what should and shouldn't be taught on college campuses.[14]

Add to these opinion poll numbers the voices from numerous contemporary commentators who argue that higher education is not delivering like it should. The *Wall Street Journal* observed, "The political pressure on higher education is rooted in a simple but vexing question: Is the government getting a good return on the money it is pouring into the U.S. college system?"[15] The answer to this question is so pressing precisely because the contemporary Commonwealth—and the nation—stand at a crossroads between divestment and reinvestment. We decide which road to take. America must understand where we've been, where we want to go, and the ways in which higher education can help us get there.

Standing at a Crossroads

According to Kentucky historian James C. Klotter, this is not the first educational crossroads Kentucky has faced. In the 1940s the state's education system "stood in shambles." While "95 percent of American children were enrolled in elementary school . . . only 63 percent of Kentucky's were." The state spent "only half the national average per child to educate its children" and "ranked dead last in high school graduates."[16] And yet, according to Klotter, things "might have been very different."[17] The state's first "real opportunity," he explains, "came in higher education" with Transylvania University.

In the early American republic, Transylvania University of Kentucky was "one of the three best colleges in the United States, and was certainly the best in the South."[18] Thomas Jefferson believed Virginians needed to improve their educational offerings or else, as he put it, "We must send our children for education to Kentucky [Transylvania] or Cambridge [Harvard]."[19] Transylvania's success was at least partly due to public support for the institution. In 1818, the education-minded Governor Gabriel Slaughter and the Democratic-Republican General Assembly voted overwhelmingly to improve Transylvania's governance in an "Act Further to Regulate the Transylvania University."[20]

The state appointed thirteen new board members, including famed Kentuckian Henry Clay. As Speaker of the US House of Representatives, Clay was instrumental in recruiting the Yale-educated minister Horace Holley to be Transylvania's president. A leading Boston minister, Holley had been serving as a member of Harvard's Board of Overseers and was already something of a public intellectual. When he accepted the job at $3,000 a year, he was one of the highest-paid presidents in the country, and seemingly overnight the reputation of the institution started to rise.[21] Three years into the job, Transylvania's enrollment was up to 282, rivaling Yale and Harvard at 319 and 286, respectively.

When Jefferson Davis—the future president of the Confederate states—was a freshman US senator, an astounding 10 percent of Senate membership consisted of Transylvania alumni.[22] Holley's vision was to transform Lexington into the "Athens of the West," and he was achieving it. Perhaps his greatest success was in recruiting faculty to campus, including Transylvania's chief of eccentricity, Constantine Samuel Rafinesque. The self-educated son of a French merchant, Rafinesque was a professor of botany and was widely known as an "erratic genius."

Popular among students, if not with the administration, Rafinesque was flanked by other important faculty such as medical professors Daniel Drake and Charles Caldwell. Both studied under famed Founder Benjamin Rush at the University of Pennsylvania. Caldwell was instrumental in securing a sizable $10,000 appropriation from the state legislature to purchase medical books from Europe. Many of the books are still at Transylvania today. Additionally, Holley built up the law school, hiring noted elected officials and judges.

Transylvania's meteoric rise, however, proved Icarian. The 1824 presidential election pitted John Quincy Adams against Andrew Jackson. Although Jackson won the popular vote, neither candidate secured a majority of the Electoral College. Consequently, the US House of Representatives decided the matter. Kentucky governor Joseph Desha and the General Assembly instructed Kentucky's delegation to vote for Andrew Jackson. At the bidding of Henry Clay, however, the delegation defied Desha and instead voted for John Quincy Adams, who won the presidency.

Desha was incensed by Clay's defiance. Viewing Transylvania as a surrogate for Clay, Governor Desha directed his ire at the school's president, Holley. In a scathing address to the General Assembly, Desha attacked Holley and Transylvania, accusing the school of becoming elitist and misusing the state's funds. His indignation and rhetoric convinced the legislature to sever support. Dejected by the attack, Holley "finally resigned under pressure, the school lost momentum, and perhaps the state's best chance for a world-class university had passed."[23] Although Transylvania continues to educate an important cohort in Kentucky, few would say it ever recovered its former status within American life.

Fast-forward two centuries, and the Commonwealth is once again endowed with remarkable institutions of higher education, including a resurgent, and fully private, Transylvania University. But, Kentucky's public higher education is yet again experiencing cuts.[24] As a state and a nation, we must course correct—we must choose the road reminiscent of Kentucky statesman Henry Clay.

Higher Education and the New American System

During his long tenure as the ideological head of the Whig Party, Henry Clay championed what he called the "American System." Elegant in its simplicity, but comprehensive in its scope and ambition, the American System proposed economic and social policies aimed at stimulating commerce and diminishing regional strife. It sought to establish a protective tariff, a central bank, and internal improvements funded through public land sales.

Clay first began using the term "American System" in the mid-1820s. But his full legislative vision for the system would play out over the next decade. One example was Clay's 1833 Distribution Bill. The bill, which was vetoed by President Andrew Jackson, proposed using money from public land sales for infrastructure and education.[25] Now long forgotten, the failed legislation laid the groundwork for the Morrill Land-Grant Act of 1862, a seminal bill for public higher education that we discuss in greater detail throughout the book.

Not unlike the Distribution Bill and the other American System legislation, the Morrill Land-Grant Act distributed to each state endowments of land to be sold and used for the "support, and maintenance of at least one college."[26] Named after Senator Justin S. Morrill, a northern Whig-turned-Republican who championed the measure, the legislation in many ways reflected Henry Clay's vision to fund education and infrastructure.

The original land-grant universities went on to graduate countless civil servants, business leaders, and luminaries in the arts and sciences. By conservative estimates, alumni include more than 500 Rhodes Scholars, 500 federal legislators, 200 governors, and a handful of US Supreme Court justices, vice presidents, and foreign heads of state. Over the years, hundreds of Pulitzer Prize winners and Nobel Laureates have affiliated with these institutions as students, professors, and researchers. Currently, the CEOs of Apple, Walmart, Ford, Verizon, BP, Berkshire Hathaway, McKesson, and Koch Industries— eight of the globe's largest companies—are land-grant alumni. The schools have aggregate endowments that total more than $64 billion, and annually they educate nearly two million students.[27]

The land-grant schools were also instrumental in training military officers who served in the Spanish-American War, World War I, and World War II. President Dwight D. Eisenhower bore witness to the "efficacy of that training" and the "great services" the land-grant officers "rendered to the United States of America on the field of battle."[28] In addition to military training, land-grant scientists engaged in agricultural and engineering research that aided national efforts.

If there is any didactic lesson from the passage of the legislation, perhaps it is the courage shown by President Abraham Lincoln when he signed the measure only weeks before the deadly Civil War battle, Antietam. Today, Kentucky and the nation require bold action in the face of mounting challenges. To paraphrase Confederate general Thomas Jonathan "Stonewall" Jackson—who fought for the South at Antietam—Kentucky must not take counsel from its fears.[29] Brave leaders such as Justin Morrill, Henry Clay, and Lincoln believed internal improvements to roads and waterways were needed to stimulate the economy—but the internal improvements we most need today are to the state's human resources, to the development of human intellect that will allow the Commonwealth and America to thrive in a knowledge economy.

Society has spent years building up pensions, unemployment benefits, and other important societal safety nets. While these programs are commendable and necessary, to succeed going forward America must also shift resources toward proactive programs that equip citizens for lives of self-reliance and fulfillment in a competitive global environment. Funds should go toward equipping young people and striving learners of all ages—especially the most vulnerable—to navigate a complex economy; in addition to treating the symptoms of society's ills, communities must strive to engage in preventative medicine.

Many are justifiably skeptical about whether higher education is worth increased public investment. But in the next seven chapters, we outline the benefits of higher education, the micro- and macroeconomic impacts of universities, and the ways in which Kentucky's universities sustain basic societal functions, as they train doctors, nurses, surgeons, lawyers, judges, social workers, mental health professionals, teachers, engineers, journalists, architects, researchers, first responders, and ministers, among others. Equally important, we explore the ways in which our universities spark society's "creative class" and preserve the humanities, incubating new innovators, artists, and entrepreneurs who rejuvenate industry.

We examine studies that detail the "soft" benefits of an educated populace. College graduates, for example, have higher levels of political participation and better health habits; they are less likely to commit crimes and are more likely to pay their taxes and become involved in local churches, social causes, and charities.[30] As Kentucky is increasingly globally connected, universities can also provide a critical link to the world as a tool for diplomacy.[31]

In short, stronger colleges mean a stronger society, and now, more than ever, the Commonwealth needs to reinvest.

What Does Our Book Add to the Current Conversation?

This book addresses a decade-long cacophony that describes, decries, dissects, and attempts to cure higher education's putative "crisis." In some ways, we are reacting against recent titles such as *Academically Adrift: Limited Learning on College Campuses* (a study on the surprising lack of learning taking place on many college campuses); or *Higher Education?: How Colleges Are Wasting Our Money and Failing Our Kids—And What We Can Do about It* (a book that exposes colleges' challenges and proposes some solutions); or *The Innovative University: Changing the DNA of Higher Education from the Inside Out* (a tome that offers dire prophesies about academic institutions that do not embrace innovative disruption); or *Declining by Degrees: Higher Education at Risk* (a book that also addresses higher education's pressing problems); or, *Education's End: Why Our Colleges and Universities Have Given Up on the Meaning of Life* (an assessment of the moral gap that universities are failing to fill in modern society).[32]

The aforementioned titles are just a snapshot of the contemporary landscape of chatter about higher education. The books reflect real, and in some cases valid, sentiments concerning universities today. Fully 96 percent of senior university administrators and 89 percent of US adults believe that higher education is in "crisis"; and, what is worse, almost four in ten deem the crisis "severe."[33] Some of these prognostications are accurate, but many are simply hyperbolic. Higher education faces very real struggles. But most Americans still sense the benefits of college; 94 percent of parents "say they expect their child (or children) to attend college."[34] And, in the marketplace, college training is more valuable than ever. The unemployment rate for graduates of four-year colleges hovers around a remarkably low 2.5 percent.[35]

While we do not dismiss the real and important challenges that face the academy (we address some of the more salient issues in chapter 6), our work primarily serves as a counterpoint to the din of discourse decrying the "crisis." College continues to provide immense benefits within the democratic tradition. We build on the work of Matthew T. Lambert's *Privatization and the Public Good: Public Universities in the Balance,* which traces the privatization of higher education; we similarly advocate for greater collaboration between private and public sectors, in an acknowledgment of the growing connections between higher education, private industry, and the public sector.[36]

Lambert's work details the public misunderstanding of the work of the university and of the general motives of faculty and administrators. Meanwhile, the motives of public representatives may also be misunderstood, given the current perceived attitudes of state officers toward funding higher education, especially in Kentucky. One aim of this book is to help stimulate better communication between the academy and the state's public servants. Our hope is that, by detailing the benefits that the academy offers society, elected officials and others can cultivate a fact-based confidence that investment in public higher education is an investment in the state's future human capital.

Throughout the book we draw on the recent scholarly essay collections *What is College For?: The Public Purpose of Higher Education* and *To Serve a Larger Purpose: Engagement for Democracy and the Transformation of Higher Education.*[37] These collections explore ways in which colleges can increase community involvement and infuse campus life with civic-minded missions and culture. Recent works written in defense of liberal arts and liberal education, including Michael S. Roth's *Beyond the University: Why Liberal Education Matters* and Martha Nussbaum's *Not for Profit: Why Democracy Needs the Humanities,* inform our thinking on the broader societal role of the university and its unique place within the republic.[38]

Professor Charles Dorn of Bowdoin College, in his work *For the Common Good: A New History of Higher Education in America,* looks back over two centuries to quote from Joseph McKeen's inaugural address in 1802: "Literary institutions are founded and endowed for the common good, and not for the private advantage of those who resort to them for education." So even while colleges and universities continue to seek the next great technological innovation and develop graduates prepared to compete in a global workforce, they must never lose sight of how these endeavors support the ideals espoused by McKeen. By so doing, concludes Dorn, our universities foster the "civic capability and commitment to the public good necessary for American democracy not to simply survive but to flourish."[39]

These and other works make compelling philosophical arguments for the relevance of a liberal education. In this book we make a similar case tailored to these times and the unique situation facing the Commonwealth. Rather than focusing exclusively on a liberal education, we put forward a defense of the university as an institution that (flaws and all) lends indispensable support to civil society, the economy, and our culture. Using Kentucky-specific history as case studies, we explore topics that are, nonetheless, nationally relevant.

For a modest state—both in terms of size and population—the Commonwealth has at times exerted an outsized influence and has produced an ample share of noted political figures. Mere weeks after the start of the Civil War, native Kentuckian Abraham Lincoln wrote to Illinois senator O. H. Browning in 1861: "I think to lose Kentucky is nearly the same as to lose the whole game." Although there are obvious differences between the Kentucky of today and the Kentucky of yesteryear, much can be extrapolated from the experience of Kentucky as it relates to the role of public higher education in the United States.

The Commonwealth is at a crossroads, but so is the nation. Looking to the past and understanding the present provides perspective that can guide the state's future path. In chapter 1 we chronicle the history of American higher education and detail its timeless role in elevating democracy. Chapter 2 explores the ways in which higher education shapes students into productive, prosocial citizens. Chapter 3 examines the Fourth Estate and the role the university plays in improving and reforming local and national governance. Chapter 4 discusses universities as global bridges that attract international talent and facilitate goodwill across continents, countries, and local communities. Chapter 5 examines the irreplaceable role of the liberal arts and the humanities in a holistic educational experience. Chapter 6 addresses some of the pressing challenges universities face and potential paradigms for discovering solutions. And chapter 7 outlines four institutions in Kentucky—two public and two private—that provide examples of unique approaches to collective problem solving.

In constructing our argument, we highlight the work of Charles Sabel, a professor at Columbia University and a former MacArthur Fellow. Sabel's ideas regarding the reinvention of mass production and its ramifications for modern welfare democracies inform the way higher education can likewise reform and improve while it still delivers essential services.[40]

We do not overlook the serious difficulties that higher education must confront; but we emphasize the need to leverage and magnify the great good higher education offers, even as schools make institution-specific reforms. At their best, universities prepare citizens for sustained engagement with today's economy and democracy. Whatever the academy looks like in twenty years, that role is unlikely to change. But for the academy to play its part, investment is required. And for Kentucky, instead, to divest is a retreat from the globally competitive environment that it must embrace. To do otherwise than engage that environment may leave the next generation ill-equipped for the world they are poised to inherit. The work of the university is in many ways the work of civil society; from teaching trades and disciplines to enhancing social exchanges and leadership capabilities, it is, quite literally, the preventative medicine for some of society's most vexing sicknesses. Our analysis, which intersperses Kentucky history and case studies with statistics and trends, suggests that one of the best paths for Kentucky's progress continues to be robust investment in the citizenry of the Commonwealth through education.

We again invite readers to pose the same question asked by the *Wall Street Journal*: "Is the government getting a good return on the money it is pouring into the U.S. college system?"[41]

This book makes a case, but also encourages you to judge. Does Kentucky's constellation of public institutions of higher learning merit divestment or increased investment? Stakeholders and investors in higher education—including taxpayers and lawmakers—should think critically about how higher education might achieve greater dividends for the Commonwealth. But they must do so with a full understanding of the best that higher education has to offer.

Universities face challenges. But challenges also present opportunities. With public support, higher education can reform itself and improve in important ways while continuing to prepare students for productive citizenship and full participation in the local economy. In 1835, Henry Clay was disappointed in President Jackson's decision to veto legislation for internal improvements. "If the bill had passed," he said, some "twenty millions of dollars" would have gone to "internal improvement, [or] education."[42] He continued: "What immense benefits might not have been diffused throughout the land by the active employment of that large sum? . . . How many youthful minds might have received the blessings of education and knowledge, and been rescued from ignorance, vice, and ruin?"

How many minds, indeed?

ONE

The Democratic Ethos
of Higher Education

The link between democracy and higher education has long been embedded in the American story. In this chapter we explore the evolution of the university in the United States and Kentucky by highlighting four figures (George Washington, Justin Morrill, Sarah Blanding, and Harry Truman) whose histories detail higher education's public purpose.

The modern university was once dubbed "a series of separate schools and departments held together by a central heating system." And, in a play on this line, "a series of individual faculty entrepreneurs held together by a common grievance over parking."[1] Whether parking, heating, or, today, WiFi, such tongue-in-cheek caricatures belie a more serious worry that higher education is rudderless and lacks a unifying raison d'être. Across the United States, pockets of politicians view higher education in rather narrow terms; they seek to peg public funding, for example, to the size of postgraduation salaries or other criteria that are ostensibly focused more on outcomes than on inputs.[2] Many professors and administrators, at times at odds with this perspective, see the cultivation of critical thinking as college's central purpose.[3] Meanwhile, student feedback demonstrates the role that social relationships play in university life.[4] These and other visions of higher education may initially appear to conflict; in reality, they often operate in concert to serve higher education's broad public purpose.

In Derek Bok's *Higher Education in America,* the former president of Harvard University divides the historical aims of the American academy into several distinct periods. "Until the Civil War," he writes, "most colleges in this country [had] only one aim—to educate an elite group of young men for the learned professions and positions of leadership in society." Institutions such as Harvard and Yale strove to "discipline the mind and build the character of their students" through "strict disciplinary code[s]" and "compulsory attendance at chapel."[5] In the early years of the Republic, however, this monolithic, largely ecclesiastical, form of education began to abate. By the mid-nineteenth century, new ideas about the role of college gained support.

As industrialization and agriculture expanded, demand increased for training in the so-called practical sciences. Benjamin Franklin and the leaders of what became the University of Pennsylvania, in anticipation of this shift, founded an institution to teach "those things that are likely to be most useful," in addition to the "most ornamental."[6] This kind of vocational-minded schooling would later inspire the Morrill Land-Grant Act of 1862, which subsidized the creation of public agricultural and industrial colleges across the United States. In the late nineteenth century, other pragmatic programs were launched in "domestic science, engineering, business administration, physical education, teacher training, and sanitation and public health."[7] Around the same time, historically black colleges and universities (HBCUs) were founded as a result of the Second Morrill Act of 1890. The act required states either to eliminate race as part of admissions criteria or to provide a separate state-sponsored institution for African Americans.[8]

Universities also began more rigorous scientific research. In 1873, the wealthy bachelor Johns Hopkins bequeathed his fortune to fund a college that made its purpose the discovery of new knowledge.[9] Other schools such as Harvard and the University of Chicago followed by awarding PhD degrees and engaging in extensive scientific inquiry. The American research university was born.

Today, many postsecondary schools trace their origins to one or more of the aforementioned movements. In narrating the sweeping origins of contemporary American higher education, writers tend to overlook the democratic ethos woven into this history. We highlight the figures of George Washington, Sarah Blanding, Justin S. Morrill, and Harry S. Truman and discuss their visions of how higher education might foster democratic engagement, raise the country's global reputation, cultivate goodwill among states and nations, and expand opportunities for more Americans. From the founding years of the early Republic, to the Civil War and World War II, they lived during some of America's most tumultuous times. Their efforts solidified the democratic purpose of colleges and even today still lend insight into how higher education can regain its footing and increase opportunities for those from all economic backgrounds.

George Washington and the National University

Some of America's greatest proponents of public higher education were themselves not college graduates. Harry S. Truman was the only US president of the twentieth century without a college degree, but he nonetheless established the highly influential Commission on Higher Education and helped administer the GI Bill. These initiatives marked "a substantial shift in the nation's expectation about who should attend college."[10] Likewise, US senator Justin S. Morrill of Vermont, a self-educated merchant, championed legislation that helped establish public universities in every state. George Washington's schooling was limited when compared with some of his political peers, but he became one of the early Republic's most prominent proponents of a national university and, among the founders, was arguably second only to Thomas Jefferson in promoting civic-minded postsecondary education.[11]

From the beginning of Washington's presidency in 1789 to the end of his life in 1799, the establishment of a national university was a reoccurring focus for him. He publicly promoted the idea and donated seed money to start it.[12] Washington's rhetoric on the subject suggests that he hoped a national school would assuage intercolonial discord and ensure that education of the nation's future leaders would follow a uniquely American political curriculum. In his mind, to protect liberty, it was as vital to teach republican principles and constitutional governance as it was to maintain a skilled army.

Washington's own lack of formal education likely influenced his crusade to secure for others (albeit exclusively white males at the time) the opportunities he himself never received. Not attending college was, according to one biographer, "a deficiency that haunted him throughout his subsequent career."[13] Jefferson, for example, studied at the College of William & Mary and read law under the famous George Wythe; John Adams attended Harvard and learned law from John Putnam; James Madison went to the College of New Jersey (now Princeton) and spent a postgraduate stint studying with the school's president, John Witherspoon. Both Alexander Hamilton and John Jay attended King's College (now Columbia). Haunting or not, Washington's academic background differed from those who advised him, but he still understood and appreciated the role his colleagues' education had on the nation's founding.

The idea of a national university was initially discussed by Benjamin Rush and, later, by the delegates at the Constitutional Convention in 1787; but it was eclipsed by other pressing matters. Washington, however, resurrected the proposition throughout his presidency.[14] In his First Annual Message to Congress he observed, "There is nothing which can better deserve your patronage than the promotion of Science and Literature." The acquisition of knowledge, he continued, was the "surest basis of public happiness" and was essential to the "security of a free Constitution."[15] Whether Congress should help support existing schools or fund a new national university he left to their discretion. Yet, four years later, in correspondence with Adams, he was unequivocal that "a national University in this country is a thing to be desired."[16]

Washington again returned to the idea in his Eighth Annual Address to Congress: "I have heretofore proposed to the consideration of Congress, the expediency of establishing a National University; and also a Military Academy." As he saw it, the former was important not only for "National prosperity and reputation" but also to prepare the "future guardians of the liberties" in the "science of Government." Meanwhile, the military academy would secure freedom through creating "an adequate stock of Military knowledge for emergencies."[17]

Washington wished to insert similar ideas in his canonical Farewell Address, but Hamilton—who helped draft it—thought the proposal was best discussed in his annual message to Congress.[18] For his part, Washington continued to promote the plan well into retirement and went so far as to bequeath "fifty shares which I hold in the Potomac Company . . . towards the endowment of a UNIVERSITY to be established within the limits of the District of Columbia."[19]

Congress eventually enacted the proposal for a military academy in 1802, but Washington's dream of a national school never came to fruition. This is not so surprising given the politics of the day; the newly created government had little power to tax, which resulted in only meager revenues to spend on federal projects. Early legislation that assisted some state governments to support and fund public education locally may also have contributed to the new republic's failure to charter a national school.[20]

The Northwest Ordinances of 1785 and 1787, two of the few legislative successes of the Confederation Congress, paved the way for new states to enter the Union. The 1785 ordinance specified that a section of each new township should be rented to a settler whose payments were to fund and maintain public schools.[21] The desire for public schooling was further emphasized in the 1787 ordinance, which declares that in the new territory, "Religion, morality, and knowledge, being necessary to good government and the happiness of mankind, schools and the means of education shall forever be encouraged."[22] These laws could help explain how townships and states, rather than the national government, assumed the task of providing public education early in the country's history.[23]

Establishment of a national university, though, remained a matter of congressional debate well into the late nineteenth century and is still discussed in some circles today.[24] Washington sensed that public postsecondary institutions could benefit students, boost prosperity, enhance the nation's global standing, and help diminish provincial tendencies. Along with Rush, Jefferson, Madison, and others, he understood that higher education was a public good that could shape the futures of those who would guard the nation's civil liberties.

Morrill and Universities for Students of Toil

More than half a century after Washington's death, Congress passed what is perhaps the single most significant piece of legislation for the democratization of higher education. The Morrill Land-Grant Act of 1862 apportioned to each state endowments of land to be sold and used for the "support, and maintenance of at least one college" that—without excluding classical studies—would focus mainly on agricultural and mechanical arts, as well as military instruction. Its impact on the provision of "liberal and practical education" tailored for the "industrial classes" was, to put it mildly, far-reaching.[25]

Few in Congress foresaw the long-term significance of the measure when it was passed amid the turbulence of the Civil War. If anyone sensed its importance, however, it was Morrill, the congressman who championed the act. Born in 1810 in Strafford, Vermont, Justin S. Morrill came from hardscrabble circumstances and had little formal schooling. He received a basic elementary education and then attended local academies (akin to high schools) for two terms. On the advice of his lifelong mentor Judge Jedediah H. Harris, Morrill took a job as a local merchant's clerk. Though his formal schooling ended early, he was a lifelong autodidact. He borrowed books from Harris on "the History of England, Thomas Jefferson's Notes on Virginia, the Federalist, and various Sir Walter Scott and James Fenimore Cooper novels."[26] While working in Maine he took a class in bookkeeping and devoted his Sundays "to study or general reading." He later reflected that it took "a long time and much labor" to gain the education he acquired and that "it was a great disadvantage to me that I could not go to school."[27]

His initial arguments for the "college act" in the US House of Representatives centered on the economic gains that would come by way of better agricultural education. "Other nations lead us . . . in nearly all the practical sciences which can be brought to aid the management and results of agricultural labor," he lamented. "We owe it to ourselves not to become a weak competitor in the most important field where we are to meet the world as rivals." He also made a moral appeal for the measure: "We have schools to teach the art of manslaying and make masters of 'deep-throated engines' of war, and shall we not have schools to teach men the way to feed, clothe, and enlighten the great brotherhood of man?"[28]

In the Senate, Morrill found an ally in Iowa Republican James Harlan. As if to complement Morrill's arguments, Harlan discussed how the measure also expanded opportunities for working-class citizens. "The passage of this bill will be one step in the right direction," he said to the Senate. "It will be, in effect, a declaration that Congress will no longer discriminate against the people; that the masses, on whose shoulders have been imposed the burdens, shall participate in the enjoyment of some of the advantages of Government."[29] The measure passed both chambers, but President James Buchanan vetoed the bill on constitutional grounds—Congress, he felt, did not possess the power to intervene so directly in the state's affairs.

Later, as a member of the Senate, Morrill introduced a revised version of the bill in 1862. In light of the Civil War, the new bill provided that the colleges would teach military tactics as well. Morrill once again marshaled arguments about national competitiveness and the need to stave off the deleterious effects of soil depletion. This time he also pointed out that the bill was an attempt to make education affordable to America's "sons of toil." Harlan similarly defended the measure as a way to help "the children of the nation." The bill passed and was signed into law by President Abraham Lincoln just weeks before the battle of Antietam, the deadliest day of the Civil War. As one historian put it, the Land-Grant Act "forced education to fit the changing social and economic patterns of an expanding nation. It helped to create equality of educational opportunity by offering education at public expense to the industrial classes; it gave some measure of dignity to the vocations pursued by such classes."[30]

The Land-Grant Act also proved important to the country's military efforts beyond the Civil War. Officers from the schools served in the Spanish-American War and World War I. In the early twentieth century, the campus programs evolved into the now-familiar Reserve Officers' Training Corps (ROTC). With the outbreak of World War II, thousands of ROTC officers helped in America's initial mobilization. A decade later, President Dwight D. Eisenhower bore witness to the "efficacy of that training" and the "great services" the officers "rendered to the United States of America on the field of battle."[31] In addition to military training, land-grant scientists engaged in agricultural and engineering research to aid the war effort. Thanks to the Servicemen's Readjustment Act of 1944 (known today as the GI Bill) these schools would greatly expand as they provided an educational landing place for thousands of GIs returning from World War II.

Sarah Gibson Blanding and the Truman Commission

In 1943, the American Legion promoted legislation that eventually became the GI Bill. The primary author of the legislation was American Legion leader Harry Walter Colmery. Pitched as a "square deal" for veterans, the bill included, among other benefits, unprecedented educational subsidies for the nation's returning veterans. The measure passed unanimously through both chambers, and—one week after D-Day—President Franklin Roosevelt signed it into law.

"Ultimately," American Government scholar Suzanne Mettler writes, "more than twice as many veterans used the higher education provisions than the most daring predictions officials had forecast."[32] By the expiration of the first bill in 1956, nearly half of the sixteen million World War II veterans had received some kind of educational training through the program.[33] In 1947 alone, GIs accounted for close to 50 percent of all students enrolled in American colleges.[34] Given this remarkable growth in the nation's postsecondary numbers, President Harry S. Truman organized the President's Commission on Higher Education.

Despite having never completed a college degree, Truman, like Washington, led some of the most sagacious and well-educated minds of his age. The cabinet he inherited upon President Roosevelt's passing included Secretary of Labor Frances Perkins (a student of Mount Holyoke College, Columbia University, and the Wharton School of the University of Pennsylvania); Secretary of War Henry L. Stimson (a graduate of Yale College and Harvard Law School); Attorney General Francis Biddle (who graduated from Harvard with both undergraduate and law degrees); and Secretary of the Interior Harold L. Ickes (who did the same at the University of Chicago). While a young captain in World War I, Truman grasped the value of a college degree when—as a self-described "old rube"—he was assigned to lead infantry training for "Harvard and Yale boys."[35] Little did he know then that such experiences might come in handy for his not-so-dissimilar role twenty-seven years later.

Truman was strongly convinced that the citizenry's access to postsecondary opportunities should be expanded. In an address to graduates at Howard University, the historically black college in Washington, DC, he expressed remorse at the thought that some of the graduates might be denied opportunities to use their new skills due to racial prejudice. "I wasn't able to go to college at all," he confessed. "I had to stay at home and work on the family farm." While some are denied opportunities for "economic reasons," he lamented, still others are denied opportunities "because of racial prejudice and discrimination." He continued: "I want to see things worked out so that everyone who is capable of it receives a good education. I want to see everyone have a chance to put his education to good use, without unfair discrimination."[36] These kinds of sentiments guided the work of the President's Commission on Higher Education, which became known colloquially as the Truman Commission.

Assembled in 1946 and active until its last report in 1948, the Commission contained "outstanding civic and educational leaders," including Kentucky native Sarah Gibson Blanding. A distinguished alumna of the University of Kentucky and, later, the first female president of Vassar College, Blanding challenged women to "step up and offer opinions on matters of academic policy."[37] She noted that the key to improving American education "is to raise the level of expectancy. . . . As we expect young people to do better work, they will do the better work."[38] She sought to extend educational and employment opportunities to citizens who were traditionally excluded from that type of civic participation, including young mothers. "I think women have not fulfilled their responsibilities as citizens as they might. . . . Too few of us have the thrill of participating actively as citizens. For that reason it may be more important today to educate women than men. . . . With a little initiative and planning they could find time to do a job as citizens too."[39] Blanding envisioned a future that is increasingly being realized, one in which women attend college in larger numbers than men.

Blanding's ambitious nature and zeal for high achievement energized Truman's Commission, which was charged with examining "the functions of higher education in our democracy" as well as "the means by which [the functions] can best be performed."[40] The result was a widely praised and scrutinized six-volume report titled *Higher Education for American Democracy*. The work laid out a philosophical vision for American higher education and provided practical recommendations to confront both contemporary challenges and those on the nation's horizon. History shows that the report's actual legislative impact was minimal. Nevertheless, its foresight was significant, and many of its suggestions and predictions would eventually come to pass. And, when "viewed as the harbinger of mass higher education in the United States, the . . . report is considered one of the most influential documents in the history of American higher education."[41]

Kentucky's Council on Higher Education initiated a similar report in 1980 titled *In Pursuit of Excellence*. In it, the Prichard Committee—named after its leader and political prodigy Edward Prichard—emphasized the need for increased quality in higher education, strategic leadership, and wise use of funds; it also highlighted the need to educate for a service-based rather than a manufacturing economy.

Both the Prichard Committee and the Truman Commission reflected the symbiosis between education and the state. Where the state goes, so goes the education system and vice versa. Injure one and the other bleeds. The Truman Commission stated, "Long ago our people recognized that education for all is not only democracy's obligation but its necessity. Education is the foundation of democratic liberties. Without an educated citizenry alert to preserve and extend freedom, it would not long endure."[42]

Around the same time, and only five years before the famous desegregation case *Brown v. Board of Education*, W. E. B. Du Bois remarked, "Of all the civil rights for which the world has struggled and fought for 5,000 years, the right to learn is undoubtedly the most fundamental."[43]

These sentiments echoed those articulated in the United States more than a century and a half earlier, and yet sadly for most black Americans the struggle for equal educational opportunities had just begun. A warning in another particularly prescient passage of the Truman Commission's report bears repeating today: "If the ladder of educational opportunity rises high at the doors of some youth and scarcely rises at all at the doors of others, while at the same time formal education is made a prerequisite to occupational and social advance, then education may become the means, not of eliminating race and class distinctions, but of deepening and solidifying them."[44] Preventing this phenomenon is just as important to strengthening democracy in the twenty-first century as it was in the twentieth.[45]

Higher Education's Responsibilities to Democracy Now

For Washington and his contemporaries, the case made for higher education was not only that it could increase prosperity, but also that it could educate youth for political participation, raise the country's international standing, and diminish provincialism. For Morrill and his allies, investment in higher education promised to yield agricultural and economic returns and help the nation remain globally competitive; but, equally, it promised to expand opportunity for the "sons of toil" and help "enlighten the great brotherhood of man." For Blanding, colleges had "a responsibility to society to educate the kind of citizens who will produce the type of civilization we want."[46] For Truman and his commission, economics and global competitiveness also played a role, but more important was the way in which higher education could help sustain democracy through a greater global perspective and educational access. "Equal opportunity for all persons, to the maximum of their individual abilities and without regard to economic status, race, creed, color, sex, national origin, or ancestry is a major goal of American democracy," the report stated.[47]

Contemporary universities still aim to boost individual success. Data show that, even with troubling tuition hikes, the long-term financial returns from a college education far exceed the individual monetary investment for most students and families.[48] Colleges and universities also aim to provide high-quality general education and create a campus atmosphere that prepares pupils for lifelong civic engagement and prosocial behavior. Aside from the obvious benefits that come with having educated surgeons, judges, engineers, and others, studies suggest that those who attend college exhibit increased levels of political participation and are more likely to attend churches and become involved in various social causes.[49] As mentioned earlier, college graduates exhibit better health and contribute to the state through paying their taxes.[50] Further, they are more likely to volunteer, vote, be civic leaders, and give larger amounts to charity. They are less likely to need public aid.[51] Meanwhile, study abroad programs and international students help spread goodwill overseas as the nation's research production continues to bolster its global reputation.[52]

By these and other metrics, contemporary universities are fulfilling the democratic missions outlined by the likes of Washington, Morrill, Blanding, and Truman. Notably, however, in some areas universities are faltering and need improvement. Chapter 7 more fully details the promises and perils of contemporary higher education in this regard. A recent report by the Pell Institute for the Study of Opportunity in Higher Education says that while the rate of affluent students graduating from college has gone from 40 percent in the 1970s to 77 percent today, for low-income students the rate has only increased from 6 to 9 percent over the same period.[53] Other reports have questioned such figures, putting the graduation rate closer to 17 percent for the lowest quintile of students.[54] These and even more conservative estimates are nonetheless sobering in light of the Truman Commission's call nearly seventy years ago to expand opportunity "without regard to economic status."

Commenting on the state of inequality in the United States, the chancellor of the University System of Maryland, William E. Kirwan, recently remarked:

> Our public universities—especially our public flagship campuses— have the obligation to help expand access to higher education for more low-income, first-generation, and non-traditional students . . . not just those students fortunate enough to win some sort of "lottery of birth." Our flagship campuses have the broad statewide reach and historic responsibility embedded in our Land Grant traditions to take on this challenge and help reestablish the American Dream for the millions of people who have seen that dream become a nightmare. There can be no more important responsibility and calling, nor a priority more critical for the long-term success and prosperity of our state and nation.[55]

On the occasion of his retirement in 2015, after leading institutions and an entire system of public higher education for more than twenty-five years, Chancellor Kirwan—a graduate of the University of Kentucky—made this observation:

The difference in lifetime earning between having a college degree and not having a college degree is over $1 million. There's no way out of poverty without a college degree.

What is America? America is the land of opportunity, the upwardly mobile society. We are that no more. It rings hollow. Our nation and our universities have got to come to grips with this problem, and I don't think enough is being done to address this issue. Obviously we need to get greater public investment in higher education to address this issue, but higher education has to do its part. Higher education has got to become more focused on the ability to deliver lower cost, high-quality education.[56]

If our system of higher education is to live up to its legacy, to support democracy and improve the minds and lives of able and willing citizens, we must solve this challenge. The university, after all, is more than just a place for scholars to share a heating system or a common grievance over parking. It is a sanctuary of citizenship where young and old come to expand their skills, broaden their horizons, and prepare themselves for the rigors of twenty-first-century citizenship. Washington, Morrill, and Truman never graduated from college, but they appreciated better than most how the aims of democracy are inextricably tied to the nation's universities. The Morrill Land-Grant Act passed amid the Civil War, and the GI Bill was created during World War II. This history teaches us that contemporary political and economic challenges, though daunting, should not serve as an adequate excuse for jettisoning our nation's educational ideals; rather, today's difficulties should remind us just how important it is to expand and adhere to the democratic purpose of higher education.

TWO

"Univercities" and the Soul
of the Student-Citizen

The names Apple, IBM, Intel, Microsoft, and Cisco are mainstays of today's Dow Jones Industrial Average. When the Dow first appeared in 1896, however, these firms did not exist. The market was dominated by now-arcane brands U.S. Leather, National Lead, American Sugar, and Chicago Gas.[1]

By contrast, in Kentucky, Transylvania University and the University of Louisville were chartered in the 1700s and today are still going strong. Centre, Georgetown, and Berea Colleges, as well as the University of Kentucky, were founded in the 1800s. Though majors and disciplines have changed, most of these schools still occupy the same campuses. Looking beyond the Bluegrass, Harvard was chartered in 1650 and Yale in 1701. While one of the authors of this book graduated from Yale, the other is an alumnus of Oxford, chartered a few centuries earlier in 1096.

Institutions of higher education have experienced remarkable longevity. It's not clear what accounts for this endurance; but, in John Dewey's seminal *Democracy and Education* he observes that in any civilization "the achievements of the adults are far beyond what the immature members would be capable of if left to themselves." He continues: "With the growth of civilization, the gap between the original capacities of the immature and the standards and customs of the elders increases." Merely "growing up" or simply mastering "the bare necessities" does not suffice "to reproduce the life of the group." Education, therefore, "and education alone, spans the gap."[2]

Dewey's theory shares a resemblance with Aristotle's much older idea on the transmission of societal virtues. More recently, Wesleyan president Michael S. Roth has melded the ideas of Dewey with those of contemporary thinkers, such as Richard Rorty and Martha Nussbaum, to explain why the best of higher education aims "beyond the university," to educate the whole person for lifelong learning and civic engagement.[3]

To this discussion we add that the expansion of the American university into the so-called multiversity has resulted in a public-private agency that is uniquely tailored to educate the whole student and prepare him or her for contemporary citizenship.[4] And, yet, the multiversity, or what we call the uni-ver*city*, is not without flaws. Some, for example, perceive it as failing to deliver not only educational instruction but moral instruction as well.[5] For higher ed-ucation to be successful in the twenty-first century it must continue to pursue excellence in its traditional mission, but it must not neglect the equally im-portant social, spiritual, moral, and civic sides of burgeoning student-citizens. Such undertakings require investment, especially as students today appear to be confronting unprecedented emotional and mental health struggles.

Evolution of the American University

The modern flagship research university is a fascinating case study in insti-tutional evolution. During early colonial life, colleges in America focused, almost exclusively, on educating Christian white males in the classics and religion for participation in an aristocratic governing coterie.[6] Colleges drew heavily on the educational traditions of Great Britain and its associated clas-sism. As America became more diverse with a steady influx of immigrants from Scotland, Ireland, and other European countries, new perspectives on education influenced these institutions.[7] Higher education became practically minded just as research-based discoveries disrupted traditional liberal educa-tion. As America's needs and culture changed, so too did its universities. As discussed in chapter 1, the Morrill Land-Grant Act of 1862 grew educational opportunities, and institutions expanded to teach agriculture, medicine, law, and engineering. With the economic growth of the late 1800s and early 1900s, schools found financial support through generous benefactors, some oriented toward the arts and others toward scientific inquiry.[8]

According to former Columbia University provost Jonathan Cole, today's American university is in many ways an amalgam of the old German mod-el that was focused on pure research and the British model that emphasized instruction and the organization of undergraduate education.[9] The mod-ern American university, with its ever-increasing emphasis on research, was heavily influenced by Daniel Coit Gilman. Hired to run a brand-new insti-tution with an emphasis on research rather than on undergraduate teaching, the Yale-trained Gilman took the helm of Johns Hopkins University when it opened its doors in 1876. Recognizing that a top-flight university required the best faculty one could hire, Gilman set off to do just that. The roster of the fac-ulty and affiliates Gilman recruited to Baltimore is a who's who of prominent scientists and thinkers in nineteenth- and early twentieth-century America: in addition to Thomas Hunt Morgan, John Dewey, and Woodrow Wilson, there were James J. Sylvester, founder of the *American Journal of Mathematics*; Henry Baxter Adams, prominent historian; Henry C. Adams, renowned public finance economist; and Henry A. Rowland, the accomplished physicist who helped found the American Physical Society.[10]

Upon Gilman's retirement from Hopkins in 1901, Woodrow Wilson, soon to become president of Princeton University, extended this tribute to his friend and mentor:

> If it be true that Thomas Jefferson laid the broad foundation for American universities in his plans for the University of Virginia, it is no less true that you were the first to create and organize in America a university in which the discovery and dissemination of new truths were conceded a rank superior to mere instruction, and in which the efficiency and value of research as an educational instrument were exemplified in the training of many investigators. In this, your greatest achievement, you established in America a new and higher university ideal, whose essential feature was not stately edifices, nor yet the mere association of pupils with learned and eminent teachers, but rather the education of trained and vigorous minds through the search for truth under the guidance and with the cooperation of master investigators.[11]

Colleges also began to provide special military training programs, and some facilitated research in warfare. Collegiate sports blossomed as America's appetite for leisure increased and as schools valued the role of physical exercise in developing a healthy mind. The changing, multifaceted nature of universities soon led to lamentations about "a lack of consensus on clarity of mission and purpose."[12] This criticism still sounds today.

In the 1940s, the Servicemen's Readjustment Act, or GI Bill, paved the way for a dramatic increase in college enrollment, as the federal government provided financial aid to veterans after World War II.[13] The rapid expansion of colleges over the next two decades culminated in yet another wave in the 1970s. Pell Grants offered opportunities to attend college to students that demonstrated financial need. This, coupled with government investment in research, began to entangle higher education and the state in complex ways, and it created more administrative needs to assure compliance with federal demands. By the 1990s and 2000s, society shifted to actively try to increase ethnic and gender diversity on college campuses. Women became much more equitably represented in law and medical schools compared to their presence in the 1970s, and the various university forms—religious, liberal arts, research, agricultural, and vocational—converged.

The end result is what Clark Kerr christened the "multiversity." According to Kerr, the university today is a "city of infinite variety" with "many separate endeavors under a single rule of law."[14] We elect to use the more aspirational term "univer*city*"—derived from combining the Latin *universitas* (the whole) with the Latin *civitas* (citizen). During a young student's most formative years, the modern univer*city* aims to influence the whole student-citizen.

Aristotle and the Virtuous Univer*city*

The goal of human life is wisdom and virtue, according to Aristotle. The highest purpose of the city-state (*polis*) is, in turn, to craft wise and virtuous citizens. Yet, acquiring virtue is not easy. An acorn, after all, only reaches its full oak tree potential in the right conditions. So, too, a college-age youth achieves a virtuous character under the conditions of proper experience and habit. The first of these conditions is education. As Aristotle put it, "That the legislator must, therefore, make the education of the young his object above all would be disputed by no one."[15] But to what end should students be educated? Not surprisingly, on this point legislators often differ.

In Aristotle's *Ethics,* he identifies at least three kinds of knowledge: theoretical knowledge (*episteme*), skill-oriented knowledge (*techne*), and practical knowledge (*phronesis*). Each has its own purpose. Episteme, for example, is contemplative, oriented toward physics, mathematics, logic, and abstract theory. Techne is pragmatic and technically focused—centered on how to build a house or a structure. Phronesis, on the other hand, is what we associate with wisdom and virtue, the "practical knowledge" of how to act with character. This latter kind of knowledge is not abstract. Indeed, for Aristotle, it is not enough to know about virtue—instead, one must actually become virtuous.

While he acknowledges that opinions differ on what kind of knowledge should be taught, Aristotle suggests that all three have a role, but especially wisdom and virtue. The univer*city* is well positioned to transmit these kinds of knowledge, including phronesis, but not simply through a first-year ethics course. As important as knowledge about ethics and politics may be, knowledge alone is not sufficient to inculcate virtue. Aristotle states: "The purpose of the present study is not, as it is in other inquiries, the attainment of theoretical knowledge: we are not conducting this inquiry in order to know what virtue is, but in order to become good, else there would be no advantage in studying it."[16] The individual acquires virtue and wisdom through virtuously engaging in the polis or city-state, or, in the case of student-citizens, the univer*city*.

If the ideal city-state is a unique partnership in which citizens learn from society's collective virtues, for Aristotle the ideal city-state must be small enough to allow for meaningful participation in civic life. But it must also be large enough to accommodate diverse expression.[17] Not unlike a state flagship, Athens had a total population of about thirty to forty thousand residents.[18] Like the city-state, the modern university was born out of collective partnerships aimed at a communal good.

The Univercity and the State

Clark Kerr, longtime chancellor of the University of California, Berkeley, writes that the original "idea of a University" was a communal village of "priests" (think Oxford or Cambridge). Eventually, the modern university became a "one-industry town" with an "intellectual oligarchy." In the twentieth century this ballooned into a multiversity, a city of "infinite variety":

> Some get lost in the city; some rise to the top within it, most fashion their lives within one of its many subcultures. There is less sense of community than in the village but also less sense of confinement. There is less sense of purpose than within the town but there are more ways to excel. There are also more refuges of anonymity—both for the creative person and the drifter. As against the village and the town, the "city" is more like the totality of civilization as it has evolved and more an integral part of it; and movement to and from the surrounding society has been greatly accelerated. As in a city, there are many separate endeavors under a single rule of law.[19]

Given the complexity and diversity of such an institution, it is easy to see why Kerr says there may be less sense of "purpose" and "community." However, as society becomes ever more diverse and complex, higher education should respond by preparing student-citizens to navigate their postgraduation reality. This is part of the university's duty to educate the whole person for meaningful citizenship "beyond the university."

In Christopher P. Loss's book, *Between Citizens and the State: The Politics of American Higher Education in the 20th Century,* he chronicles the twentieth-century transformation of the university "into a key mediating institution between citizens and the state." As he tells it, "Higher education's promise was first glimpsed during the Great Depression. But its full potential as a tool of statecraft was not truly realized until World War II, when the state deployed education to build better soldiers and rewarded veterans with generous education benefits in exchange for their wartime sacrifices."

Legislation such as the GI Bill and the Higher Education Act "expanded educational opportunity to increasing numbers of Americans." The state, "believing that higher education created psychologically adjusted citizens capable of fulfilling the duties and obligations of democratic citizenship," further extended its reach. According to Loss, the university became the quintessential gateway to civic participation.[20]

Although Loss says this linkage has significantly declined in the last forty years, we believe a strong connection remains. Although it is statistically undeniable that contemporary higher education lacks the same level of state-based support it once had, the reciprocal relationship between citizen and state nevertheless persists. Despite tuition hikes, government-backed federal loans support most students. And, despite rhetoric regarding a student loan crisis, the long-term financial returns from a college education continue to far exceed the individual monetary investment for most students.[21]

Critiquing the Univer*city*

Of course, the ever-expanding scope of the university is not immune to criticism. And, indeed, the univer*city* has long been scrutinized. Noted American educator and Kentucky native Abraham Flexner lamented in his 1930 treatise *Universities: American, English, German* "that of Harvard's total expenditures not more than one-eighth is devoted to the *central* university disciplines at the level at which a university ought to be conducted."[22] A strong critic of sports programs and so-called practical education, Flexner insisted that inquiry, and not mere job training, was the central role of the university.[23]

Today, Flexner's critiques have become commonplace. Major public and private universities house, feed, educate, entertain, and discipline thousands of resident students. Many schools provide settings for students to socialize, exercise, and shop. Some campuses have mini-power plants, pseudo-professional sports programs, grounds' crews, maintenance staff, mail systems, printing services, police departments, investment arms, development foundations, technology transfer divisions, intellectual property offices, and dozens of lawyers, lobbyists, accountants, and public relations specialists. To some observers, these initiatives appear to be tangentially related to the faculty, who are chiefly responsible for teaching and producing research, and the students, who are there to learn.

Many today echo the sentiments expressed by Robert Maynard Hutchins, who was dean of Yale Law School and president of the University of Chicago: "It is a good principle of educational administration that a college or university should do nothing that any other agency can do as well."[24] This is sound advice. And we agree that state schools especially, as stewards of taxpayer dollars, should seek to eliminate waste and redundancy and to improve efficiency and innovation in higher education. But for the public's sake, such overtures to efficiency must not become excuses to trim the core work of the university.

The Univercity and Liberal Education

In his book *Beyond the University: Why Liberal Education Matters,* Michael Roth traces the debate over the philosophical aim of liberal education from Thomas Jefferson to John Dewey to today.[25] Jefferson, he explains, understood education as a means of guarding against tyranny and as a way to improve the nation's laws. Not unlike Aristotle, Jefferson valued the way in which the laws of the whole affected and shaped the individual's happiness. Jefferson's educational philosophy is captured in the text of his "Bill for the More General Diffusion of Knowledge."[26] "It is believed," Jefferson wrote,

> that the most effectual means of preventing [Tyranny] would be to il-luminate, as far as practicable, the minds of the people at large. . . . It is generally true that people will be happiest whose laws are best, and are best administered, and that laws will be wisely formed, and honestly administered, in proportion as those who form and administer them are wise and honest; whence it becomes expedient for promoting the public happiness that those persons, whom nature hath endowed with genius and virtue, should be rendered by liberal education worthy to receive, and able to guard the sacred deposit of the rights and liberties of their fellow citizens.[27]

Roth points out that Jefferson's fellow Founder, Benjamin Franklin, shared a more pragmatic passion for education when he established the University of Pennsylvania. He famously commented "Art is long and Their time is short."[28] Booker T. Washington may have felt similarly. Education, for him, was most centrally a means of economic and societal advancement, and his institution trained African Americans in vocational trades. Contrastingly, transcendentalist Ralph Waldo Emerson viewed education as a means of individual self-discovery, expression, and autonomy. The free individual could help advance a morally deficient society shackled by slavery. W. E. B. Du Bois, who criticized Booker T. Washington's vocational-minded education, believed that advancement and freedom were not to be found in mastering service-oriented trades but in achieving excellence in the arts and sciences and, by doing so, freeing others. William James and Jane Addams, on the other hand, saw education as good not only for achievement of personal excellence or intellectual autonomy, but for fostering societal cooperation and collective burden sharing. James also saw value in how the liberal tradition could spur creativity and imagination.

In addition to inheriting these philosophical traditions of American liberal education, the American univer*city* is also the distant product of deeply religious and morally minded institutions. As universities became allied with the state and adopted scholarly objectivity toward deity, the academy became understandably secular; yet many today lament the lost emphasis on moral instruction. *New York Times* columnist David Brooks elaborates:

> Religious rituals like mandatory chapel services were dropped. Academic research and teaching replaced character formation at the core of the university's mission. Administrators and professors dropped spiritual language and moral prescription either because they didn't know what to say or because they didn't want to alienate any part of their diversifying constituencies. The humanities departments became less important, while parents ratcheted up the pressure for career training. Universities are more professional and glittering than ever, but in some ways there is emptiness deep down. Students are taught how to do things, but many are not forced to reflect on why they should do them or what we are here for. They are given many career options, but they are on their own when it comes to developing criteria to determine which vocation would lead to the fullest life.[29]

Roth agrees. In his analysis, the modern academy tends to overemphasize intellectual autonomy and the cultivation of so-called job skills. Meanwhile, Brooks points out, technology has commoditized the mere transmission of information, and therefore, if colleges are to remain relevant "they are going to have to thrive at those things that require physical proximity. That includes moral and spiritual development. Very few of us cultivate our souls as hermits. We do it through small groups and relationships and in social contexts."[30] Though it may stumble, this is one area where the univer*city* could thrive. Although it is large, its size allows for many small groups and new experiences to live and grow under the order of the greater enterprise.

Students understand this role of the univer*city*. David Chambliss and Christopher Takacs's extensive survey conducted at Hamilton College confirms what many in higher education have long sensed, that "what really matters in college is who meets whom, and when" and that it is "the people . . . that make a difference."[31] In other words, what students and alumni value from their university experience often derives from relationships. Occasional critic of the academy and noted Harvard business scholar of disruptive innovation,

Clayton Christensen, recently observed that successful alumni who gave to their university did so because of a relationship with a single professor: "Their connection wasn't their discipline, it wasn't even the college," Christensen commented. "It was an individual member of the faculty who had changed their lives."[32]

Summarizing their findings in a *New York Times* interview, Chambliss and Takacs report that "students who had a single dinner at a professor's house were significantly more likely to say they would choose the college again" and "in learning to write, it made a lasting difference if students had at least one experience of sitting down with a professor to go over their work." To students, they recommend living "in one of the old-fashioned dorms with the long hallways, multiple roommates and communal bathroom" in order "to bump into a lot of different people every day."[33]

Chambliss and Takacs's findings support Vincent Tinto's interactionalist theory of why students drop out of college. In his widely cited *Leaving College*, Tinto analogizes the student's decision to leave college with the citizen's decision to leave society.[34] Drawing on Emile Durkheim's theory of suicide, which states that individuals who are isolated and poorly integrated into society tend to be at risk, Tinto suggests that when students are poorly integrated, they are more prone to drop out or flunk out. In college, two forms of integration take place, one academic and the other social—failure to integrate in one or both can increase the probability of departure.[35]

Part of twenty-first-century citizenship is learning to work cooperatively in a pluralistic society and understanding the historical context surrounding diverse interactions. Race, gender, and social justice are a few areas that have emerged on college campuses as societal magnets that can bring a community closer together or, in some cases, repel participants in diverging paths. To reach the ideals of the modern univer*city* and to integrate students academically and socially, residents need help to become comfortable interacting in these dynamic spaces, even if they hold different deep-seated opinions. Having such conversations requires environments where all participants feel they can have a meaningful voice on campus.

Recent analyses on race and college enrollments suggest that some campuses are finding ways to adapt the shifting dynamics of the university, while others remain in roughly the same state they were in more than three decades ago. Even with affirmative action, some of America's top universities struggle to fully integrate minority students.[36] Because contact across racial and economic divides decreases the likelihood of intergroup prejudice, society has a strong incentive to ensure that colleges help students feel comfortable interacting within the campus environment, which can serve as a microcosm of society.[37]

And so we return to Aristotle, who states in his *Ethics*: "We become just by the practice of just actions. . . . Lawgivers make the citizens good by inculcating [good] habits in them, and this is the aim of every lawgiver; if he does not succeed in doing that, his legislation is a failure. It is in this that a good constitution differs from a bad one."[38] Today, the city-state can craft ethical and productive global citizens for the twenty-first century, by properly training and educating them with such aims in mind. When a generation misses this instruction, the consequences can be dire.

Just think: Aristotle's own texts were lost for centuries before they were rediscovered in the Middle Ages. Without a mechanism to transmit not only knowledge, but morals, civic virtue, skills, political wisdom, and spiritual insight, society suffers. The university, more than any other collective agency, is the primary vessel for transmitting America's intellectual and social heritage to successive generations. We must leverage the infrastructure of the univer*city* not only to teach the good but to let students become it. "For just as man is the best of the animals when completed, when separated from law and adjudication he is the worst of all."[39]

In an age of information, the university must increasingly foster superior relationships, stimulate innovation, and, of course, prepare students for a workplace that demands lifelong learning. Inasmuch as universities succeed in this duty, there is little doubt that they will continue to be around longer than the latest stock pick du jour. As Brooks observes, "It's tough to know how much philosophical instruction anybody can absorb at age 20, before most of life has happened, but seeds can be planted. Universities could more intentionally provide those enchanted goods that the marketplace doesn't offer. If that happens, the future of the university will be found in its original moral and spiritual mission, but secularized, and in an open and aspiring way."

THREE

Higher Education and the Fourth Estate

The Commonwealth's fertile farmland is well known for sprouting spontaneous blades of bluegrass, producing Triple Crown–winning horses, and—not to be overlooked—inspiring Wendell Berry's pastoral poems. An avid agrarian and noted scholar-poet, Berry is a Kentucky original who emerged in recent decades as the nation's crunchy granola, *American Gothic* social critic. As he has unpacked America's strained relationship with its land, Berry has also directed criticism at the very institution that nurtured him both academically and professionally: the University of Kentucky. Berry's persistent critiques of the state's flagship, despite his strong ties to the school, illustrate how universities today often play patron to professorial gadflies. While it may cause headaches in front offices, it is positive for democracy when universities serve as a repository for scholar-critics who, in turn, serve a central function within the Fourth Estate.

Organic Berry

Raised in a multigenerational farming family, Berry took both his BA and MA in English from the University of Kentucky before he headed to Stanford to study under the famed western writer Wallace Stegner. After stints in Europe as a Guggenheim fellow and teaching at New York University, Berry returned home. Like his father before him—a lawyer and congressional staffer who left life in DC to farm in Kentucky—Berry took a job at the state's flagship school and swapped his life in the Big Apple for a life spent growing things like, well, apples.

As a professor, Berry continued to produce poetry, fiction, and cultural commentary. Although much of Berry's art and activism aims to harmonize human interaction with the land, his recent relationship with his former employer (and alma mater) has hardly been harmonious. Berry's approach toward the university is not dissimilar to James Baldwin's famous relationship with America: "I love America more than any other country in the world and, exactly for this reason, I insist on the right to criticize her perpetually."[1] To borrow a phrase from Proverbs, whom Berry loves he seems to chasten.

While this philosophy (I criticize because I love) is hardly sage marital advice, there is little doubt that Berry's affection for the University of Kentucky is genuine. In 2010, when Berry made national headlines for removing his personal papers from the school's library, he called the decision heartbreaking. "The university is an alma mater," he commented at the time. "I have two degrees from the University of Kentucky. I taught there. They have honored me. I have friends there; I have friends that are currently teaching there. And so this is a break that feels to me like a family disruption."[2] Some of Berry's fondest memories are tied to the institution. It was on UK's campus that he first saw his future spouse "standing by [a] wooden newel post . . . in Miller Hall."[3] Years later, during Miller Hall's renovation, the wooden post wound up at the Berry family farm as "the first thing a visitor sees when entering their home."[4]

Berry chose to withdraw his personal papers from the UK library not just because the university "accepted a $7 million gift from the coal industry and named their dormitory the Wildcat Coal Lodge,"[5] although that certainly catalyzed the decision, but also because the university chose to extract natural resources from university-owned woodlands. Berry's longtime critique of the University of Kentucky's research ambitions also played a role. As scholars Matt Bonzo and Michael Stevens explain:

> [In the 1990s] Berry decided to "quit" from the University of Kentucky to farm his land full-time, he insisted on that verb, emphatically asserting that he did not "retire" or "move on"—his point was that he could no longer identify himself with a large state university that, as he argues in *Life Is a Miracle,* fosters an "academic Darwinism [that] inflicts severe penalties both upon those who survive and those who perish. Both must submit to an economic system which values their lives strictly according to their productivity." Berry offers an even harsher assessment when he states in "Higher Education and Home Defense" that the purpose of higher education has now devolved into training for "entrance into a class of professional vandals."[6]

Paradoxically, Berry's scathing criticism in "Higher Education and Home Defense" was published around the same time that the University of Kentucky asked Mr. Berry to return to teach for them.[7]

What does this say about universities? While not a universal truth, many campuses are not afraid to recruit individuals who are active critics of the very schools that employ them or of the democratic or economic systems that support their work. Universities pay to attract top scholars, poets, social scientists, and philosophers who, not unlike Berry, may be protected by tenure, which ensures that they are free to level criticism without fear of certain kinds of retaliation. Commentator Harold T. Shapiro observes that the university helps "society as both a responsive servant and a thoughtful critic. Thus, although the modern research university must serve society by providing the educational and other programs in high demand, the university must also raise questions that society does not want to ask and generate new ideas that help invent the future, at times even 'pushing' society toward it."[8]

Berry is to the University of Kentucky what universities can be for the communities they serve—critical observers, amenders, and improvers. The likes of Berry fuel the intellectual fire at universities, which in turn help refine the decisions of policymakers. As we will explore in more depth, tenure allows professors to play the dual role of raising "questions that society does not want to ask" and generating "new ideas" without the threat of punishment or job loss. First Amendment freedoms, along with protections such as institutional autonomy and academic tenure, provide scaffolding to sustain the role universities play in a vibrant Fourth Estate.

Enlightenment and the Fourth Estate

Famously, British statesman Edmund Burke identified the three estates of parliament—the Clergy, the House of Lords, and the House of Commons; he then, according to Thomas Carlyle, observed that up "in the Reporters' Gallery yonder . . . sat a Fourth Estate more important far than they all."[9] Burke's Fourth Estate, the press, informs the public, checks government power, and shapes policy leaders and the body politic.

Adding his own gloss to Burke's observation, Carlyle writes, "It is not a figure of speech, or a witty saying; it is a literal fact. . . . [Printing] . . . is equivalent to Democracy." He continues: "Whoever can speak, speaking now to the whole nation, becomes a power, a branch of government, with inalienable weight in law-making, in all acts of authority. It matters not what rank he has, what revenues or garnitures: the requisite thing is that he have a tongue which others will listen to; this and nothing more is requisite."[10]

A free press remains a central element in America's intellectual life. Conservative jurist Robert Bork included within the so-called chattering class "university faculties," as well as "print and electronic journalists, church bureaucracies, the staffs of public interest organizations, segments of the bar, members of the judiciary, and the purveyors of cultural symbols in motion pictures and television entertainment"—essentially, any and all who "deal in the transmission of ideas."[11]

Universities Inform the Public and Check the Government

Bork is not alone in his observation that university faculties work within the Fourth Estate. From Twitter to think tanks, university-supported research and expertise frame and enhance the national conversation. Scholar Michelle Stack urges readers to think about the duo of "journalism and academe" as "networks of knowledge" as well as public spaces in which both journalists and academics facilitate society's "messy and contested" public dialogue.[12]

In addition to its role in producing and diffusing information, the university also acts as an institutional check on governmental power. Thomas Jefferson and James Madison, who had witnessed the impact of governmental tyranny firsthand, hoped to diffuse and decentralize power. In their judgment, there were few better ways to guard against abuse of governmental power than by subjecting it to the scrutiny of a free press and an informed citizenry. Jefferson wrote to Enlightenment thinker Adamantios Korais: "There are certain principles in which all agree"; they include, he continued, the "Freedom of the press." Jefferson described it as a "formidable censor of the public functionaries," explaining that, "by arraigning them at the tribunal of public opinion," the press "produces reform peaceably, which must otherwise be done by revolution. It is also the best instrument for enlightening the mind of man, and improving him as a rational, moral, and social being."[13]

Jefferson understood higher education and the press as two branches of the same melioristic tree. Regarding education, he wrote, "experience hath shewn, that even under the best forms, those entrusted with power have, in time, and by slow operations, perverted it into tyranny; and it is believed that the most effectual means of preventing this would be, to illuminate, as far as practicable, the minds of the people at large."[14] Today, the best of higher education and the best of journalism serve this dual function of "enlightening" minds and being a "formidable censor of the public functionaries."

Take "Cash for Clunkers." The program was designed to stimulate the economy shortly after the 2008 market collapse and the subsequent financial struggles of US auto manufacturers. Under the program, funded by $3 billion in federal money, drivers could exchange their cars for vehicles that were more fuel efficient and receive a $4,500 kickback. Sold to Congress and the American people as a win for the economy, the environment, and automakers alike, it was only academics who, by retrospectively analyzing the results, were able to show that the program was indeed, as some opponents suspected, too good to be true. In 2014 researchers at Texas A&M University, in conjunction with the National Bureau of Economic Research, discovered that most participants had already been planning to purchase a new car and that American auto manufacturers were worse off since participants that would have purchased more expensive vehicles instead bought less-expensive fuel-efficient cars.[15] There was of course some hope that it would help the environment, but University of Michigan researchers determined that average fuel economy improved by less than 1 mpg under the program.[16] Here, academia provided ex post analysis and the press spread the word. One headline in the *Boston Globe* read, "Cash for Clunkers: How Bad Public Policy Gets Made."[17] The important point here is not one specific program or the administration behind it but the process by which the university can work within the Fourth Estate.

In another example of the university functioning to "enlighten the mind" of the public, in the 1980s, two professors started to cull through old housing advertisements and researched historical records to track the housing market from the late 1800s to the present day. Karl Case and Robert Shiller, professors of economics at Wellesley College and Yale University, respectively, analyzed changes in home prices and identified housing bubbles. They developed a methodology known now as the Case-Shiller index to chart housing prices and predict booms and busts. Three years before the 2008 plummet in housing prices, Robert Shiller observed, "This is the biggest boom we've ever had. So a very plausible scenario is that home-price increases continue for a couple more years, and then we might have a recession and they continue down into negative territory and languish for a decade."[18] The Case-Shiller index is now a standard resource for financial analysts and policy makers.

Information hubs such as universities facilitate this kind of research that can enlighten, warn of dangers, and notify the public of policy and economic opportunities. Beyond predicting risks in home purchasing, academics illuminate the nuances of nutrition; they make known the consequences of human behavior and social habits; they unearth natural resources and find ways to optimize energy technologies; and they even engineer better traffic patterns and construction methods and materials.

One costly problem for taxpayers is road construction delays. One driver recently spoke for all of us when he said: "It's horrible. There's more traffic than ever, and it's taking forever"; another said, "It's a nightmare," and "It's a pain."[19] Inconvenience and lost productivity aside, costs associated with construction delays weigh financially on taxpayers. From 2013 to 2015, Texas expended $21.4 million beyond budget due to delays caused by unmoved utility lines. New Jersey recently lost more than $10 million from utility relocation delays. Kentucky says that over 30 percent of its projects are delayed due to utility relocation complications.[20] It turns out that an important solution for on-time and on-budget road projects is simply fluency in reading utility and highway plans.[21]

Legislators authorize road projects with the best of intentions, but in some states the relevant utility companies lack incentive to move utility lines "quicker, and [there is] no disincentive if they don't do it in a timely fashion." An academic team at the University of Kentucky interviewed officials of the Kentucky Transportation Cabinet and utility companies and analyzed successful utility relocation management teams; thanks to their efforts, legislators and developers now have a few answers that, when applied, can save taxpayers millions and enhance road infrastructure.[22] Targeted education for on-site workers is among the chief solutions. And while this not-so-new problem had been analyzed in the past by the federal government, that analysis failed to give concrete solutions beyond the recommendation of "a lot of coordination, cooperation, and communication."[23] Scholars at the University of Kentucky, however, were uniquely positioned to parse the data and provide a meaningful suggestion to ensure that highway plans were read, understood, and implemented.

The university's focus on education, objective research, and intellectual independence provides an environment where there is relative freedom to pursue inquiry. As illustrated in the foregoing examples, universities and academics provide useful information to the public and the government, support better decision making based on their research, and monitor the success or failure of policies post enactment through critical analysis. Diminished funding, however, jeopardizes the effective fulfillment of these and other roles within the republic.

Higher education is experiencing mounting political pressure to better serve dynamic job markets. While this is unquestionably a worthy goal, it should not overshadow the many important functions that universities serve within a democracy.[24] Despite their noble intentions, the actions of a growing contingent of lawmakers today seek to chip away at higher education's institutional autonomy—a key protection that allows universities to perform objective scholarship and contribute to society in myriad ways.

Chipping Away at Institutional Autonomy

Tenure as a Solution for Academic Freedom

Lawmakers in states such as Kentucky, Arkansas, Missouri, Iowa, and Wisconsin have proposed dramatic reforms or sizable cuts to university systems. Increased belt tightening presents a unique challenge to autonomy and academic tenure. Wisconsin, however, was the only state that had tenure protection written into state law. Those protections have been undermined recently through Governor Scott Walker's push to see faculty "'start thinking about teaching more classes and doing more work.'"[25] Walker initiated cuts to the state's higher education system and successfully changed the state's academic tenure policy, challenging the permanency of professor tenure. Walker's push to curb costs and enfeeble tenure drew responses in favor of and opposed to the flexing of legislative muscle over university policies. Some feared changes "could bolster the forces pushing universities to operate more like businesses, eliminating departments or courses that do not attract many students or much money."[26] Others argued that policy changes are "the latest step in an ongoing attack on the University of Wisconsin as a public good that exists for the benefit of all citizens of the state."[27] The expected fallout includes concerns over shared governance, as well as questions about faculty authority over curriculum, instruction, and research.[28]

In a piece in *Politico Magazine,* two politically conservative University of Wisconsin professors, Donald Downs and John Sharpless, spoke out about the unintended consequences of these policy shifts, stating that "as far as college campuses go, we're a rare, endangered species: two long-tenured professors who lean right and libertarian. But we're increasingly worried that in trying to take up another conservative crusade, our governor, Scott Walker, is going to silence the very voices he claims to support." Walker's goal, they observed, is ostensibly conservative: loosen tenure to save taxpayer dollars. However, as the professors point out, "without tenure protections, professors like us who fight for free speech and liberty—values Walker himself espouses—could be even more at risk of being targeted on college campuses for our beliefs."[29]

In the early twentieth century, a group of professors, including the educational philosopher and professor John Dewey, took issue with various dismissals they perceived as unjust and formed the American Association of University Professors (AAUP). They investigated terminations. For example, in 1915 the University of Pennsylvania expired the contract of Scott S. Nearing, whose teachings, which criticized capitalism and child labor, rattled influential alumni. The University of Toledo also dismissed Nearing two years later for his antiwar views surrounding US involvement in World War I.[30] Law professor James H. Brewster advocated for a miners' union on strike in 1915, and the University of Colorado relatedly ended his employment.[31] Although these examples may seem like extreme outliers from the past, today what is far more common is the soft attempt to muffle criticism or stifle an unpopular view through, for example, moving a professor off an admissions committee after a private donation to an unpopular political cause is made public. Unsettled by the risks that expression of controversial views may pose to professors, the AAUP reported their findings and asserted that "the university cannot perform its threefold function without accepting and enforcing to the fullest extent the principle of academic freedom." The AAUP continued to warn of the implications of stifled academic thought:

> Public opinion is at once the safeguard of a democracy, and the chief menace to the real liberty of the individual. . . . In a democracy there is political freedom, but there is likely to be a tyranny of public opinion. An inviolable refuge from such tyranny should be found in the university. It should be an intellectual experiment station, where new ideas may germinate and where their fruit, though still distasteful to the community as a whole, may be allowed to ripen until finally, perchance, it may become a part of the accepted intellectual food of the nation. . . . One of its most characteristic functions in a democratic society is to help make public opinion more self-critical and more circumspect, to check the more hasty and unconsidered impulses of popular feeling, to train the democracy to the habit of looking before and after.

It concluded by recommending a system of tenure "to render the profession more attractive to men of high ability and strong personality."[32] Subsequently, the AAUP's 1940 statement calls for a determination of tenure after a probationary period of less than eight years.[33]

Since its inception, opinions about what tenure is and how it should be applied have been mixed. Tenure, it has been argued, creates "the intellectual vitality needed to foster great debates and important new discoveries."[34] It has served as a bulwark against administrators, legislators, and corporations with their own agendas.[35] Some see academic freedom as merely a perk of the profession, but academic freedom is also important so faculty members can share in governance, make curriculum and pedagogy decisions, and set ambitious research agendas consistent with their expertise.[36]

Tenure matters because it allows universities to recruit and retain exceptional faculty and, through them, attract economically and socially valuable grants.[37] It provides protection against "being fired for unpopular ideas, like climate change or income inequality—or for opposing the views of politicians or powerful donors."[38] Students are served through tenure protections, as a university can develop "a stable foundation of faculty who maintain academic programs, advise students, and serve the institution to improve its quality, to implement new initiatives, and to assess its effectiveness. . . . Tenure maintains that foundation of faculty personnel who have made the same level of commitment to the institution that it has made to them."[39] And despite the cobbling together of rare out-of-context examples exploited in the service of a biased perspective, "the overwhelming majority of faculty members at our best universities and colleges are highly self-motivated individuals who strive to produce new, important discoveries, and to write books that will redefine their fields well after they receive tenure."[40]

While tenure has historically provided protection for academic freedom on the back end of a career, it may have, nonetheless, the unintended consequence of inhibiting it on the front end. An academic may, for example, withhold important views, in fear of being denied tenure by politically motivated reviewers. Or, those awarding tenure may deny it to a rising academic who challenges an administration. English professor Frank Donoghue writes, "If, indeed, probationary faculty have that freedom from recrimination, then what additional freedom do they gain by being tenured? . . . For the conventions of tenure that we all know actually take away academic freedom from those with less than seven years' service [typical probationary period] at an institution."[41]

Another critic of tenure complains, "The trouble is that professors get their tenure by *suppressing* the expression of unpopular expression, not *in order to express* unpopular opinion. . . . The modern university, by its conservative inertia, has become the most hostile place for pursuing the truth. And tenure, once deemed precious, has become the most wasted, irrelevant principle."[42] Some critics call tenure an anachronism that impedes progress and stifles responsiveness in a fast-paced world of information.[43] Some say it supports a lazy practice, hinting that experienced researchers lack the inclination or ability to keep up with current trends or employ contemporary practices.[44] Even the more diplomatic of forecasters wonder whether tenure, and the long careers of those who earn it, unnecessarily limits opportunities to adapt, thus potentially sacrificing the university's "two fundamental missions of advancing knowledge and disseminating it."[45]

On balance, however, tenure has historically done a fair job of protecting professors in the pursuit of truth from dismissal, except in instances of unprofessional behavior, serious budget cuts, or apparent ineptitude. There have been exceptions in the past century, especially during the Red Scare, but the norm has been toward free inquiry. Of course, altogether shielding the tenure system from continued review and scrutiny would ironically violate the principles of free inquiry upon which the idea of tenure is founded. And, indeed, at times there are valid reasons for institutions to revise tenure policies. But, as a society, it's important to remember that a lack of protection for academics can stifle diverse views and the open exchange of ideas over time. Tenure continues to be the norm because it tends to work. Tenure's role in helping produce serious inquiry free of reprisal, as originally declared by the AAUP, is still worth supporting. Its apparent limitations and the possibility that it serves more as a recruiting tool than as a medium for free thought are rightly prompting ongoing discussions about potential new approaches.[46] However, the offer of job security as a means to attract capable scholars to freely pursue their teaching and research agendas should not be entirely overlooked or dismissed in discussions about the future of higher education and understandings of tenure.

University Freedom from Undue Outside Influence

In addition to chipping away at tenure, politicians may sometimes feel tempted to use funds as a carrot or a stick to influence curriculum and scholarship at universities.[47] Some have begun to threaten university endowment funds as a way to influence such institutions. These issues are complex, and certainly public officials as well as donors, alumni, students, staff, faculty, and parents all deserve a seat at the table when it comes to shaping the university community.

Philanthropists have recently sought to make it more difficult for schools to jettison donor intent. Billionaire Bernard Marcus of Home Depot and mutual-fund magnate John Templeton, along with others, founded the Center for Excellence in Higher Education, a nonprofit that helps "advise donors on how to attach legally enforceable conditions to their gifts." The idea, according to the *Wall Street Journal*, is to "curb colleges' discretion in spending donors' contributions." The paper quoted the senior vice president of the Templeton Foundation, Charles Harper, who states bluntly, "Anybody who trusts a university on a handshake is a fool."[48]

This should not be an either-or situation. Aligning donor intent with university needs is perhaps the most important work of public/private partnerships and will likely remain central to the future financing of higher education. Most university development offices seek unrestricted funds that the university can use for everything from supporting low-income students to paying the electric bill. While donors feel their donative intent is too often pushed aside, excessive restrictions can sometimes constrain the work of a university and, in rare cases, can raise "basic questions about academic freedom and institutional autonomy."[49] Legal claims regarding infringement of academic freedom primarily arise in three contexts: "claims of professors against faculty colleagues, administrators, or trustees; claims of professors against the State; and claims of universities against the state."[50] Rigid donor intent has the potential to jeopardize both individual academic freedom and institutional autonomy.

The threat of cutting endowments has caused some to spend more on science research, out of fear that if productivity cannot be tied to quantifiable

scientific advancements, then public officials will threaten funds. Senator Or-
rin Hatch and other members of the Senate Finance Committee asked "the nation's richest colleges and universities for details about their multibillion-dollar
endowments."[51] The federal government subsequently passed tax reform that
targeted elite private school endowments, imposing a "1.4 percent excise tax
on investment income at private colleges with an enrollment of at least 500
students and with assets valued at $500,000 per full-time student." Universi-
ty of San Diego professor Victor Fleisher has gone even further, arguing that
Congress should "require universities with endowments in excess of $100 mil-
lion to spend at least 8 percent of the endowment each year. Universities could
avoid this rule by shrinking assets to $99 million, but only by spending the
endowment on educational purposes, which is exactly the goal."[52] Journalist
Malcolm Gladwell, a longtime critic of "elite" academic institutions, says that
some universities should voluntarily relinquish their tax exemption.[53] It's fair
to examine endowments; however, when the squeeze is put on institutions
through limits on endowments or funding cuts or through onerous donor intent restrictions, this can start to exert undue influence on university speech
and scholarship and chip away at an institution's ability to play its important
independent role within the Fourth Estate.

After the Center for Excellence in Higher Education was launched in 2007
(aimed at curbing "colleges' discretion in spending donors' contributions"[54]),
a representative of the American Association of University Professors said the
organization was "very worried" that as major donors increasingly seek tighter
controls, they could begin to, whether intentionally or not, influence the ideological orientation of academic programs and classes.[55] Not everyone believes
this is a negative, as some feel that higher education lacks ideological balance.
And, because no one is forced to accept a gift, they question whether there
really is an issue of academic freedom.

While universities generally choose which gifts to receive and which to
reject, in some instances (especially those that end up in litigation) there are
complicating factors. For example, institutions change. A gift given today may
no longer be attractive for either side down the road. In the case *Tennessee Di-
vision of the United Daughters of the Confederacy v. Vanderbilt University,* Vanderbilt wanted to change the name of a building called "Confederate Memorial
Hall." The university no longer wanted an explicit relic of the Confederacy on
campus; yet the law ruled the name would have to stay—donor intent. Similarly, *William Robertson, et al. v. Princeton University* argued that donors did not
feel that the university aims aligned with the donor's original goals. These and
other cases show that although a gift may be freely given and received at one

time, the donor or the recipient can evolve. What type of protection should the state afford public, and perhaps even private, institutions in this regard?

The Supreme Court case *Sweezy v. New Hampshire* established the precedent for academic freedom protection under the First Amendment.[56] Scholar J. Peter Byrne observes that the case represents "the pressures placed on universities during the McCarthy period."[57] In the case, the Supreme Court blocked California's attorney general from barring a university lecturer in the state's system from discussing specific political content in the classroom. "The essentiality of freedom in the community of American universities is almost self-evident," the court observed:

> No one should underestimate the vital role in a democracy that is played by those who guide and train our youth. To impose any strait jacket upon the intellectual leaders in our colleges and universities would imperil the future of our Nation. No field of education is so thoroughly comprehended by man that new discoveries cannot be made. Particularly is that true in the social sciences, where few, if any, principles are accepted as absolutes. Scholarship cannot flourish in an atmosphere of suspicion and distrust. Teachers and students must always remain free to inquire, to study, and to evaluate, to gain new maturity and understanding; otherwise our civilization will stagnate and die.[58]

Writing in a concurrence to the majority opinion, Justice Felix Frankfurter argued for the "exclusion of governmental intervention in the intellectual life of a university," an opinion which in many ways has had a more lasting influence than the majority opinion.[59] Frankfurter did not invoke the Constitution or depend on the "internal system of academic freedom nor on any collateral legal doctrines."[60] Rather, he relied on the statement that endorsed the "'four essential freedoms' of a university—to determine itself on academic grounds who may teach, what may be taught, how it shall be taught, and who may be admitted to study."[61] The idea has stuck.

The Supreme Court would eventually tie academic freedom to the First Amendment, albeit somewhat loosely.[62] In support of the contention that academic freedom is indeed constitutionally protected, Professor Byrne writes that the intellectual mission of the university should be protected but that the "peripheral university functions" must not be protected. If protected, he reasons, they "will create an unwholesome incentive for school officials and entrepreneurs to use the university form as a vehicle to carry out new and additional economic activities. Universities already struggle to reconcile their intellectual missions with many schemes used to raise the funds to carry out that mission."[63]

This argument seems sound enough, but it fails to consider that the intellectual mission is often highly dependent on many of the economic and "peripheral" university functions. There is no easy rule here. But policy makers and donors should be mindful of how money can be used to foster and expand robust academic freedom, and conversely, how it can be used as a way to censor or silence speech on university campuses. Sadly, in the race to innovate and educate, cuts to state appropriations have negatively impacted the academy in this regard.[64] In the introduction, we discuss the example of Transylvania University and leader Horace Holley. It took only one antagonistic governor to cut the school's funding and drive out the school's leader with whom he disagreed. The institution never fully recovered.

If academic freedoms are not protected, both through policies and through the ability to acquire and use funds with a modicum of institutional autonomy, the university will struggle to fulfill its function within the Fourth Estate. It must be free to rigorously expose poor public policy, seek truth, and, where necessary, criticize governmental institutions. Sensitive politicians and politically minded donors may see this autonomy as insubordination or ingratitude; however, time has shown that autonomy is essential to protect and sustain the overall health and function of a stable democracy. In a commencement speech at Bellarmine University, Wendell Berry directly addressed "research universities" that "no longer make even the pretense of preparing their students for responsible membership in a family, a community, or a polity." The public benefits when universities support social critics such as Berry who deliver sharp barbs at the very institutions which nurture them; society wins when universities have the freedom to follow truth, wisdom, and conscience wherever they lead.

FOUR

Universities as America's Ambassadors-at-Large

In one of his last public lectures before his passing in 2009, former university administrator Chase Peterson discussed America's so-called deficits. From trade deficits and student achievement deficits to the federal budget deficit, he lamented that America was losing ground. He observed, however, that one area in which America had no such global deficit was higher education.[1] Despite daunting challenges, American colleges and universities rightly garner global accolades for unrivaled research, and they continue to attract some of the brightest international students. Sadly, in recent years, reports show a dip in foreign student enrollment in domestic universities. Some administrators attribute the slump, in part, to more hostile political rhetoric toward immigration.[2] And yet, thousands of students still come to study and often find employment which allows them to stay for good, leavening the economy and democracy. Other students often return home as allies, regardless of whether they go on to help shape global politics or focus on impacting their own communities.

While here, international students help prepare their domestic peers for an ever-more-global economy. Cosmopolitan curricula, language training, and international experiences also contribute. These elements and more serve as national "soft power," turning universities into ambassadors-at-large around the globe.[3] Although few notice the role universities play in foreign affairs, George Washington understood "the expediency of establishing a National University" for, among other reasons, "National . . . reputation."[4] The legacy of such a vision continues.

Global Politics and Policy: Kentucky to Korea

Not many travelers in Incheon International Airport in Seoul, Korea, are bound for Kentucky's Bluegrass. In 2010, however, that was Sung Chul Yang's destination; the former South Korean ambassador to the United States came from Korea's capital to America's "horse capital" for his induction as a member of the University of Kentucky's Hall of Distinguished Alumni.[5] Forty years prior, Yang was a freshly minted PhD from Kentucky's political science program. After stints on the faculty at Eastern Kentucky University and his alma mater, the University of Kentucky, Yang left the United States for Seoul with his sights set on political life in his home country.

From the mid-1990s until his appointment as ambassador to the United States in 2000 (one of the nation's top diplomatic posts), Yang served as a member of Korea's unicameral legislature. A tireless advocate for building a unified South Korea and North Korea, he served as president of the Unification and Policy Forum and vice chair of the Unification and Foreign Affairs Committee. Later, as ambassador to the United States, he promoted President Kim Dae-Jung's "Sunshine Policy," calling for the use of persuasion before power in dealings with neighbor North Korea.[6] Though the policy's legacy is mixed, it reinfused the region with hope and won President Kim Dae-Jung a Nobel Prize in the process. For his part, Yang was uniquely positioned to promote South Korean policy in America while he communicated the United States' concerns about condoning North Korea's human rights violations and nuclear ambitions.

Of course, not all international students aspire or ascend to such lofty political heights in their home countries; Ambassador Yang's story, however, is not anomalous. At least anecdotally, commentators have observed that international students seem to "have a higher likelihood of obtaining influential positions in their host nations."[7] Then-chancellor of the College of William and Mary, and former US Defense Secretary, Robert Gates, described having observed throughout his career the value of international exchanges in fostering amicable relations. "Connecting students across borders is one of the most effective ways of building understanding across nations," he remarked. "We never know when and where America will need allies in this world, and no program is more successful at making friends than education in the United States."[8]

Such sentiments harken back to Washington's initial premonitions that a national university would help eradicate parochial strife. He theorized, "The youth or young men from different parts of the United States would be assembled together, and would by degrees discover that there was not that cause for those jealousies and prejudices which one part of the Union had imbibed against another part: —of course, sentiments of more liberality in the general policy of the country would result from it."[9]

Believing that the students of a national university would "be at the head of the [councils] of this country in a more advanced stage of it," Washington saw the intimacy of a university experience as a way to diminish provincialism in the Republic.[10] Studies support what Washington sensed; face-to-face exchanges are an effective means to overcome bias and misperception.[11] Consequently, some scholars go so far as to suggest that educational exchanges are one of America's best routes for twenty-first-century diplomacy.[12] Certainly, educational and other exchanges helped Ambassador Sung Chul Yang bridge the gap between Kentucky and Korea; yet, exchanges are just one means by which universities influence global politics and policies for the better.

Chicago to Chile

On September 11, 1973, Chile experienced a harrowing coup d'état that ushered in the violent military junta of strongman Augusto Pinochet. In his seventeen-year reign as dictator, Pinochet carried out untold human rights atrocities and pilfered millions from the Chilean people. Like other "generals who seize power," Pinochet started out by running "the economy as a centrally directed, military-type system," writes noted economist Gary Becker. But, after serious setbacks the dictator turned toward "free market policies," as promoted by a group of Chilean economists, who came to be known as the "Chicago Boys."[13] According to Milton Friedman, who had taught some of the Chilean economists at the University of Chicago, Pinochet chose the group more by accident than acumen. The Chicago Boys were some of the only economists around without ties or loyalties to the previously ousted regime.

The group included Chileans who had graduated from Harvard, MIT, Columbia, and, of course, the University of Chicago; together they shared a conviction that Chile's unique economic problems (including its hyperinflation) would be best solved through gradual deregulation, privatization, and the expansion of American-style markets.[14] By most measures, the change was a success, and the results came to be known as the "Chile miracle."

In about two decades, the country went from having approximately half of its citizens living below the poverty line to only about one-fifth. Today, fully 85 percent of Chile lives above the poverty line (the highest percentage in South America). Few critics dispute the nation's stunning turnaround, even as some contend that Chile's economic policies caused sharper inequality and others caution against assuming that deregulation and privatization is always a guaranteed economic panacea. Although the legacy of the Chicago Boys is forever tainted by the atrocities carried out by the military junta for whom these Chilean economists worked, Gary Becker and others contend that the group's "willingness to work for a cruel dictator and start a different economic approach was one of the best things that happened to Chile."[15] Friedman observes that "in the end the central government, the military junta, was replaced by a democratic society. So the really important thing about the Chilean business is that free markets did work their way in bringing about a free society."[16] Today, despite recent setbacks, Chile is still perceived as one of the least corrupt nations in South America and one of the most economically stable.[17]

Similar stories are told about other areas of the globe. In Indonesia, another group of American-trained economists, the so-called Berkeley Mafia, orchestrated a turnabout in the country's economy during the 1960s. It is not only American-educated economists who come through in moments of crisis; when American officials were "trying to broker a deal to end the bloody 20-year civil war between Sudan and South Sudan in 2005, they had an in with the elusive guerrilla fighter leading the south's shadowy rebel forces." It just so happened that the guerrilla leader, John Garang, was a graduate of Grinnell College in Iowa. Not all US college graduates embrace American culture or economic policies, but, as one commentator observes, "A surprising number of politicians, diplomats, lawmakers, military leaders and business tycoons from around the globe—in countries both friendly and hostile—have spent time in U.S. colleges and universities," and more often than not it is a win for diplomacy, democracy, and the American academy.[18]

The Growing Number of International Students

When Sung Chul Yang attended the University of Kentucky, South Korean students were something of a rarity. Now there are more than 68,000 South Koreans studying on campuses across the United States, and today colleges are more international than ever.[19] According to the *New York Times*, in 2013–2014 "colleges in the United States enrolled a record 886,052 foreign students, an increase of 8 percent over the previous year." Most recent numbers in 2017 show a dip despite the long-term trends. Citing a joint report from the Institute of International Education and the US Department of State's Bureau of Educational and Cultural Affairs, the *Times* writes, "China remains the dynamo of global-student mobility," sending more than 274,000 students.[20] India came in second with 102,673, and South Korea third with 68,047 students studying in the United States.

Significant increases in recent years also have come in the number of students from Saudi Arabia, Brazil, and Kuwait, all of which have national scholarship programs that give students the opportunity to study beyond their borders. Saudi Arabia sent 53,919 students—an increase of nearly 20,000 from the previous year. The Middle East and North Africa now supply the fastest growing pool of international students. Iran, for example, sent 10,194 students to study in the United States and has a long history of sending students for graduate training in America. The *Atlantic* pointed out during the Obama presidency that "Hassan Rouhani, Iran's president, has more cabinet members with Ph.D. degrees from U.S. universities than Barack Obama does. In fact, Iran has more holders of American Ph.D.'s in its presidential cabinet than France, Germany, Italy, Japan, Russia, or Spain—combined."[21]

Commentators speculate whether the "Iran Nuclear Deal" would have come as far as it did if not for the significant number of high-ranking Iranian officials who graduated from US schools (most notably MIT).[22] In 2013–2014, the United Kingdom sent 10,191 students across the pond; Canada and Japan sent 28,304 and 19,334, respectively. While it is certainly positive that allies continue to send their students to America, there is perhaps more potential for positive outcomes from exchanges with not-so-friendly nations.

Assistant Secretary of State for Educational and Cultural Affairs, Evan M. Ryan, argues, "International education is crucial to building relationships between people and communities in the United States and around the world." He contends, "Only by engaging multiple perspectives within our societies can we all reap the numerous benefits of international education—increased global competence, self-awareness and resiliency, and the ability to compete in the 21st century economy."[23] Beyond assuaging discord and overcoming prejudice, there are equally valuable economic impacts from international students studying in the States.

The Economic Impact of International Students

In 2014, the National Association of Foreign Student Advisers (NAFSA) estimated that international students brought in $192,544,000 to Kentucky's local economy through a mixture of tuition expenses, living expenses, and money spent for dependents or by visiting family.[24] According to the Open Doors 2014 report, nearly three-quarters of international students receive most of their money from sources outside the United States, either through family and personal funds or assistance from home governments.[25] Citing estimates from the US Department of Commerce, the same report says that, in the aggregate, international students boost the US economy to the tune of $26.8 billion per year, translating into roughly 340,000 jobs.

While this annual windfall is significant, the long-term economic ramifications of hosting international students may be even greater. According to a 2014 Brookings Institution Study, foreign students pursue science, technology, engineering, mathematics (STEM) and business degrees at higher rates than US students. STEM and business courses attract two-thirds of foreign students compared to only 48 percent of their US counterparts.[26]

According to Brookings, almost half of foreign students work in the metropolitan areas around their universities after graduation by extending their visas under the temporary Optional Practical Training program. From these data points, the report recommends that more metropolitan business leaders "should emulate leading practices that capitalize on the knowledge and relationships of foreign students to strengthen local economies" while simultaneously "maximizing students' educational and professional experiences in the United States."[27]

Foreign students become an important link between college campuses and the world beyond. Schools already tap into this kind of exchange by having local businesses utilize foreign talent. Since the late 1980s the University of Southern California's Marshall School of Business, for example, has required its international MBA students in their twelve-month program to interface with local businesses. Students analyze potential foreign markets and deliver a strategic plan for local businesses that desire to export. The businesses benefit from bargain consultancy services and the students grow from real-world experience and networking opportunities.[28]

International Contributions to Classrooms and Campus

Apart from benefiting the US economy, international exchanges enrich the classroom and campus. With the advent of globalization, learning about the broader world while at college is a bipartisan priority for a sizable majority of Americans.[29]

On this point, Professor Susan Pearce of East Carolina University observes that "international students contribute to higher education by exposing [Americans] to information and perspectives that we may otherwise have missed. My own international graduate students offer language skills that I do not possess and insights into data sources and academic literature from their home countries."[30] Scholar Stuart Anderson reminds readers that "the United States has the enormous international advantage of being able to attract talent in science, technology, and engineering from all over the world to its most prestigious institutions. . . . The country is certainly better off by having the whole world as a potential supplier of highly talented individuals rather than only the native-born."[31]

While the benefits are abundant, hosting international students on US campuses can carry potential risks as well. In 2016, the *New York Times* reported on the dilemma that Western Kentucky University faced when it realized that an incoming wave of international students wasn't academically prepared to meet the rigors of the university's curriculum. A partnered recruiting office in India had used persuasive marketing techniques to attract locals looking to study in the United States. Promising large scholarships and immediate offer letters, the agency recruited dozens of students to travel to Kentucky's third-largest state school. According to the *Times,* 106 of 132 students recruited by the foreign office failed the school's required English skills test.[32] For Western Kentucky, this kind of recruitment of international students, seen as a pleasant opportunity for cultural exchange, led to trouble. In an age of budget cuts, universities benefit from foreign students who pay full tuition.[33] Although this example highlights a potential pitfall with exchange programs, administrators and legislators can come together and find solutions to ensure that the boon of accommodating students from other lands is not buried beneath unchecked practices.

Despite this cautionary tale in Kentucky, hosting students in the States facilitates culturally enriching experiences to the majority of American students who either cannot afford to or choose not to study abroad. And, of course, it provides immense opportunities for those qualified students who come to study in the United States from across the globe. Professor Pearce highlights other program ideas that can bring cultures into the classroom. "Even in a resource-rich country like in the United States, a very small percentage of students can afford to travel abroad to attend a university, even for a short time," she notes. "Recognizing this problem and the value of such exchanges in an increasingly globalizing world, my university, East Carolina University, created the Global Classroom, which uses the latest communication technology to establish video- and computer-linked classroom experiences."[34] It is beneficial to implement these kinds of ideas and expand study abroad programs for lower-income students in order to create a learning environment that fosters twenty-first-century citizenship.

Fulbright and the Diplomatic Vision for Study Abroad

Lest we forget, international exchanges are a two-way street, and an ever-increasing number of American students are learning abroad. Though some students are drawn to the pleasures of travel, the educational and diplomatic benefits are equally compelling. President Truman assembled his Commission on Higher Education to "insure that higher education shall take its proper place in our national effort to strengthen democracy at home and to improve our understanding of our friends and neighbors everywhere in the world."[35]

Or, as Truman phrased it in his address to the United Nations, "If we do not want to die together in war, we must learn to live together in peace."[36]

A junior senator from Arkansas and contemporary of Truman, J. William Fulbright also observed the need to improve international relations; he devised a way to do so while capitalizing on United States–owned war property left abroad after the war. Fulbright, a former president of the University of Arkansas, proposed leveraging the surplus foreign properties and the postwar debts owed to the United States to fund an education exchange program with other countries. The senator's bill succeeded, and President Truman signed it into law in 1946. Its purpose was to foster "international good will through the exchange of students in the fields of education, culture and science."[37] While the Fulbright scholarship program rollout was initially slow and belabored, a subsequent piece of legislation resolved currency issues, and by 1948 its first class had 85 participants. According to the Bureau of Educational and Cultural Affairs, the effects of the exchange were immediate, as evidenced by increased fluidity of international negotiations.[38] In Fulbright's vision of the program, it would promote positive stewardship of US properties as it helped Americans learn about individuals in other countries and enhanced global understanding of Americans.

A Harvard lecturer and administrator of the Fulbright program, Francis A. Young, saw firsthand in the 1960s the fruitful nature of the education exchange program. He observed: "The basic functions of educational exchange from a foreign policy standpoint are to broaden the base of relationships with other countries, reduce tensions, lessen misunderstandings, and demonstrate the possibilities and values of cooperative action. In short, educational exchanges pave the way for closer and more fruitful political relations. Rather than following political diplomacy, educational diplomacy normally precedes or keeps step with it, opening up and nourishing new possibilities for international cooperation."[39]

Fulbright participants from foreign countries also attest to the positive effects of the program. Internal research reveals that 99 percent of international participants report a better grasp of America and its culture; 96 percent highlight their experience on social media or other outlets; and 89 percent indicate that their educational exchange in the United States facilitated assumption of leadership roles in their home countries.[40] In addition to the Fulbright, myriad other scholarships (both private and public) facilitate international educational experiences. Prestigious awards include the Marshall Scholarship (supports American students studying at any school in the United Kingdom), the Rhodes Scholarship (supports American students studying at Oxford), the

Gates Scholarship (supports American students studying at Cambridge), and now the Schwarzman Scholarship (hosts 200 scholars annually from the United States, China, and elsewhere for a one-year master's program at China's Tsinghua University).

To say that international exchanges have proliferated in recent decades is an understatement. In 2013, some 289,408 American students went abroad for academic credit—a record high. The number more than doubled from fifteen years earlier, according to the Open Doors report. Important, though, are the almost 90 percent of domestic students who do not have the opportunity to travel abroad, whether for financial or other reasons.[41] Though it may seem cliché, learning and navigating a different culture can be a life-enhancing experience. Both the authors attest from their own personal experiences, and from witnessing the experiences of numerous students, that studying abroad expands horizons and changes lives in prosocial ways. Research suggests a correlation between studying abroad and employability, academic achievement, graduation rates, and graduating on time.[42] Studying abroad also appears to help students mature and learn to navigate novel circumstances.[43] Of course, some students—and program faculty—will regrettably approach short-term study abroad programs as "extended vacations," where diligent studying takes a backseat to sightseeing. Nevertheless, for those committed to fulfilling academic requirements while breathing in the essence of a different culture, such opportunities to travel can lead to invaluable contributions in future academic and career successes. Thus, continuing to expand the ability of students from all financial backgrounds to study abroad should remain a priority for American universities.

In addition to these programs, foreign scholars and faculty visit campuses for teaching stints, sabbatical semesters, and academic conferences. Many of these opportunities lead to longer-term relationships between scholars and institutions. Indeed, some ambitious universities have increased their international footprint with foreign facilities. Harvard, for example, has "16 officially recognized overseas offices," with three more in the works for Beijing, Cape Town, and Mumbai.[44] While Harvard's large footprint overseas may be the exception rather than the rule, they have yet to follow their peer institutions in the dramatic step of opening up an overseas undergraduate institution. Duke-Kunshan University, for example, is now operating in China; Yale-NUS College is in Singapore; and New York University has campuses in Abu Dhabi and Shanghai. The success of these institutions as global ambassadors is yet to be fully measured; however, the leadership at these schools see promise more than peril in these opportunities abroad.

US Universities Attract Some of the World's Brightest

The advent of prestigious US universities building abroad is in many ways yet another move to capitalize on international cachet. Students across the globe continue to flock here, so why not allow more to attend closer to home? George Washington speculated that a national university would boost America's reputation, and international rankings prove his point. Studies from inside and outside the United States—using various metrics—universally recognize the quality of American higher education (especially its marquee research universities).

The *Academic Ranking of World Universities* (ARWU) 2015—which ranks global universities based on "alumni and staff winning Nobel Prizes and Fields Medals, highly cited researchers, papers published in *Nature* and *Science,* papers indexed in major citation indices, and the per capita academic performance of an institution"—places 33 American universities within the top 50 globally (and 16 of the top 20 universities).[45] The London-based *Times Higher Education* World University Rankings uses a slightly different methodology and ranks 28 American universities (many of them the same) within their own top 50.[46] In 2014, *U.S. News and World Report* released its first "Best Global Universities" survey, in which it adjusted the criteria for its undergraduate rankings, such as graduation rates and admissions selectivity, and instead focused on research production, number of citations, and reputational surveys data, among other criteria. The result was what they characterized as the "Global 500." Sixteen of the top 20 and 32 of the top 50 were American universities. Of the 500 universities, 134 were from the United States. The University of Kentucky fell within the top 300 and University of Louisville within the top 500. Behind the United States, the next country with the most universities ranked was Germany with 42; yet, only one German university ranked within the top 50, University of Munich (48).[47]

In the "Global Employability Survey," conducted by a Paris-based human resources firm, researchers asked more than 4,500 global employers from twenty countries, including recruiters and managers, to rank universities. US-based universities represent 45 of the 150 on the list. England was the next closest with 13 schools listed. The publication *QS Top Universities* has slightly more than half of their top 20 and 18 of their top 50 from the United States. They base rankings on employer and academic reputation, as well as factors such as student to faculty ratio, number of international faculty and students, and faculty citations.[48] One 2009 study conducted exclusively by Chinese scholars included 17 American universities among the world's top 20 most distinguished research institutions.[49] Such overwhelming international recognition for the caliber and reputation of American universities undoubtedly makes an important impact in America's foreign policy. Yet, lest American academics become jingoistic, Derek Bok reminds us that international rankings rarely gauge the quality of education or teaching. He fears that in the battle over research and scholarly production, student learning and engagement can take a backseat.[50] While acknowledging these challenges, the success of American universities in terms of research and reputation is unrivaled.

The Korea Connection

When Sung Chul Yang received his PhD in 1970, not much commerce passed between Kentucky and Korea. Today, however, the state is home to Korean-owned auto-parts supplier INFAC North America Inc., a company that has done well enough in Kentucky to outgrow its original fifty-two-thousand-square-foot facility in Campbellsville. It recently built a new one-hundred-thousand-square-foot facility, which expanded its capacity to manufacture control cables for brakes and transmissions.[51] In July 2015, the firm announced a subsequent expansion.[52] Other South Korean firms have manufacturing operations in Lexington, Louisville, and Florence.[53] Furthermore, if we had scattered a few glossy photographs throughout the pages of this book, it probably would have been printed and bound by PACOM Korea Inc., a South Korean printer preferred by the University Press of Kentucky for its photo-infused manuscripts.

The real telltale sign, however, that even a land-locked state like Kentucky is saturated in global commerce is Kentucky's bourbon business. According to recent reports, "Kentucky produces 95% of the world's bourbon supply," and in fact "more than 5.3m barrels of bourbon are maturing in Kentucky, outnumbering the state's population." Many of those barrels are headed overseas, "with exports projected to top $1.02bn for 2014." Once again, "the latest sales figures underscore Kentucky bourbon's emergence as a 'global force.'"[54]

A global-oriented education is not just important to learn how to ask an Asian business partner what Kentucky bourbon he or she prefers. Rather, it is essential to twenty-first-century citizenship. Whether in nonprofit, for-profit, or government work, the world is increasingly connected. Universities must play a role in bringing foreign students and scholars to classrooms and campuses across the Commonwealth; they must also ensure that students of all backgrounds can explore different cultures and countries and act as micro-ambassadors for American ideals throughout the globe. This will only better equip students with the acumen to venture into the expanding global economy.

When Sung Chul Yang served as Korea's ambassador to the United States, he helped promote the country's "Sunshine Policy."[55] The policy's name comes from Aesop's fable, "The North Wind and the Sun." As the story goes, the North Wind and the Sun were quibbling over who was stronger; suddenly a cloaked traveler walked by. The Wind and Sun agreed that whoever could get the traveler to remove his cloak was mightiest. When the Wind blew hard against the traveler's cloak, the traveler only clutched it harder and closer to his body. When the Sun simply shined its rays at the traveler, he swiftly removed the garment. Fulbright and Truman understood that educational exchanges play a part in diplomacy precisely because, like Aesop's Sun, they persuade us to remove that which cloaks us in prejudice and engage in mutually beneficial exchanges and fellowship. With the continued support of generous donors, American voters, and state and federal officials, universities can persist in expanding these opportunities.

FIVE

A Liberal Education as Part of a Publicly Minded Education

University-affiliated museums, theaters, performance halls, and the students who perform in them help bring local communities together in ways that bolster civil society, enhance empathy, and grow communities. But in addition to the enhancement of local cultural offerings, the reach of liberal and performing arts and a liberal education extend well beyond weekend campus events and choir concerts.

After dropping out of college, a shaggy-haired, self-described hippie started "dropping in" on a Reed College calligraphy course. The student was Steve Jobs. Few today would tout calligraphy as a prized credential to impress prospective employers. Jobs admitted as much: "None of this had even a hope of any practical application in my life."[1]

The founder of Apple, however, would later credit the calligraphy class with changing the face of computers. In his 2005 Stanford commencement address, he recalled: "Ten years later, when we were designing the first Macintosh computer, it all came back to me. And we designed it all into the Mac. It was the first computer with beautiful typography. If I had never dropped in on that single [calligraphy] course in college, the Mac would have never had multiple typefaces or proportionally spaced fonts. . . . Of course it was impossible to connect the dots looking forward when I was in college. But it was very, very clear looking backward ten years later."[2]

Thus began Apple's quest to make computers friendly and accessible—devices that felt comfortable to have in your living room.

Before Apple, computers had appeared to many as inanimate collections of circuits and chips, plastic and pixels. A few decades later, Jobs's devices felt so intimate that they fit naturally into one's palm or pocket. One journalist reflected on his first impression of the Macintosh, exclaiming, "There were typefaces! . . . Here was a computer that treated fonts as art, not just a clump of pixels."[3]

A cynic might view this talk of fonts, calligraphy, and computers as an overemphasis on the trivial. Yet, to others such testimonials highlight the secret to both Apple's success and, perhaps more importantly, America's economic development. So, what's the special Applesauce? According to Jobs, it was the synthesis of technology and humanities, the splicing of science and art.

During Apple product launches, Jobs would conclude with a slide "of a street sign showing the intersection of the Liberal Arts and the Sciences."[4] He said at his last public product launch, "It's in Apple's DNA that technology alone is not enough—it's technology married with liberal arts, married with the humanities, that yields us the result that makes our heart sing."[5]

Jobs would say to his biographer Walter Isaacson, "I always thought of myself as a humanities person as a kid, but I liked electronics." Later Jobs read a quotation from his hero Edwin Land, the longtime CEO of Polaroid, about the "importance of people who could stand at the intersection of humanities and sciences."[6] It was after hearing that line that, as Jobs put it, he knew what he wanted to do—to stand at that intersection.

Isaacson explains, "It used to be common for creative people to stand at this intersection [of humanities and sciences]."[7] People such as Benjamin Franklin, Thomas Jefferson, and Albert Einstein are examples. Today, the sophistication of scientific experimentation and the specialization of humanities sometimes act as an unfortunate barrier to fruitful synergies. And yet, if one trusts employer survey data, this crossover of science and liberal arts has never been in higher demand. Universities are uniquely, perhaps perfectly, positioned to help inculcate these highly coveted skills in students and help foster them among faculty.

To make this point with greater vigor, this chapter illustrates the democratic value of a liberal education, discuss the contemporary perception that a liberal arts education leads to diminished job opportunities relative to other majors, and challenge this perception with growing evidence that, in fact, employers want to hire employees with humanities training precisely because it increases economic value.

Humanities Elevate Our Democratic Society

Making Life Humanly Relevant

Too many Americans live in fear, discomfort, abusive homes, poverty, or addiction. This was the reality of J. D. Vance. A product of Middletown, Ohio, and Jackson City, Kentucky—in the heart of coal country—Vance grew up in poverty. His memoir, *Hillbilly Elegy*, details how he overcame many of the vexing circumstances he experienced and eventually graduated from Ohio State University and Yale Law School. Today he is a father, a husband to a former US Supreme Court clerk, and a successful investment executive. As he tells it, Vance's path to a better place stems largely from taking personal responsibility for his education and his life, despite the social decay that surrounded him.

But his story also touches on the power of education and the cultural influences of faith, family, and service in the armed forces—all of which helped instill in him a desire to pursue higher endeavors. "Mobility isn't just about money and economics, it's about a lifestyle change," he says. In high school, when living with his mother became unbearable, Vance fled to his grandmother's care. Her priority of purchasing "a graphing calculator" over "nice clothes" influenced Vance's understanding of the value of education: "It forced me to engage with school in a way I never had before."[8]

Vance's high school performance landed him admission to the Ohio State University (OSU), but, intimidated by the cost and financial aid applications, Vance pursued the Marines instead. The tough but productive lifestyle of hard work, discipline, and self-respect in the Marines further refined his independence and set his sights on preparing to live out his personal "American Dream." The memoir, a "tough love" critique of some aspects of coal-country culture, is now a *New York Times* best seller.

Vance's memoir brings the important perspective that community and culture matter in combating today's social ills. But, as many of the best critiques of Vance's work point out, systems—economic and, especially, educational—have a significant effect on culture, community, and family life. Improvements in both spheres are required. The skills that Vance learned in the Marines, in the classrooms of OSU, where he studied philosophy, and at Yale, where he studied law, cultivated the level of self-expression, critical analysis, and intellectual rigor that helped him add his personal perspective to the national conversation. What humanities do best, after all, is humanize.

A liberal education and the humanities provide stories, such as Vance's, that deepen the soul and, ideally, increase empathy. In the words of Steve Jobs, the humanities are a part of what makes "our hearts sing." And, in the context of Vance's book, they help readers' hearts understand; Vance's clear-eyed assessment of the plight of his community and his illustration of how to course-correct reveal the power the humanities and education can offer to individuals and society.

Symbiotic Relationship of Humanities and Democracy

In American democracy the right to choose is of paramount importance. Although high schools cannot (and should not) force each and every student to attend college, they can make it easier for able students to elect postsecondary educational experiences. They can provide information and shape students' decisions by helping them understand the probable consequences of their choices. Vance appreciated this opportunity: "Whenever times were tough—when I felt overwhelmed by the chaos and instability of my youth—I knew that better days were ahead because I lived in a country that allowed me to make the good choices that others in my neighborhood hadn't."[9]

Undoubtedly, if each individual in such circumstances would obtain some level of success through education or vocational training, society might improve. We recognize hurdles that many Americans face. How can people feed their intellect when their stomachs are empty? If sustaining life becomes all-consuming, the allocation of time and money to education may seem impractical.

One of Vance's teachers recalls the impossibility of a promising student's home circumstances. When he hadn't shown up to school for a few days, she drove to his house and "found him and his seven siblings home alone, her . . . student [was] too preoccupied with tending to his brothers and sisters to care much about school."[10]

Or consider Vance's mother—once at the top of her high school class. As a teenager she was thrust into the realities of sustaining not only her own life but that of a child. Her life might have been improved if she had had, for example, the network and resources to secure an education while raising a child. Our democratic values of free choice can lead to both elevated and, sadly, to difficult circumstances—it is the pursuit and internalization of wise and informed choices that lead to desirable outcomes. We won't always make the best choices, whether intentionally or not, but if lawmakers and individuals apply the information that the best of the humanities and liberal education provide, we may be better equipped to make life choices that lead to fulfillment, flourishing, and personal and societal advancement.

Important books such as *The Grapes of Wrath* and *To Kill a Mockingbird* put contemporary issues into perspective and inform personal values. History and art provide context and an outline of ideas, providing students with answers based on human experience. We learn not only how to live, but why.

The value of a liberally educated populace is codified in federal law:

(3) An advanced civilization must not limit its efforts to science and technology alone, but must give full value and support to the other great branches of scholarly and cultural activity in order to achieve a better understanding of the past, a better analysis of the present, and a better view of the future.

(4) Democracy demands wisdom and vision in its citizens. It must

therefore foster and support a form of education, and access to the arts and the humanities, designed to make people of all backgrounds and wherever located masters of their technology and not its unthinking servants.[11]

Consider the case of countries that have had science-heavy educational curricula but now see the value of the humanities in education. As Martha C. Nussbaum describes: "They have concluded that the cultivation of the imagination through the study of literature, film, and the other arts is essential to fostering creativity and innovation." She observes, "We in the U.S. are moving away from the humanities just at the time that our rivals are discovering their worth." The humanities develop empathetic and socially aware thinking, which facilitates ideas crafted with one another in mind. The open flow of ideas and stories through free speech and a free press facilitates an informed public that is more able to promote policies based on mutually beneficial values and to select government leaders that will carry them out. Nussbaum concludes, "To keep democracy vital, we urgently need the abilities that the humanities foster."[12]

Daniel Pink observes this shift in valuing the humanities in Japan: "Japan, which rose from the ashes of World War II thanks to its intense emphasis on [left brain]-Directed Thinking, is now reconsidering the source of its national strength. Although Japanese students lead the world in math and science scores, many in Japan suspect that the nation's unrelenting focus on schoolbook academics might be an outdated approach. So the country is remaking its vaunted education system to foster greater creativity, artistry, and play. Little wonder. Japan's most lucrative export these days isn't autos or electronics. It's pop culture."[13]

J. D. Vance's grandmother, instrumental in nudging Vance toward an education, grew up in relative economic stability. Her family was able to work in Midwestern factories. Today, economic opportunities in manufacturing are too sparse to sustain the population that once relied on them. And yet, at exactly the time when the options advanced by education are needed most, attaining a postsecondary education is often economically out of reach for middle-class and economically strained families. Perhaps counterintuitively, a liberal education can be part of the solution as liberal arts and STEM fuel new opportunities in today's economy.

Astrophysicist Adam Frank writes:

In spite of being a scientist, I strongly believe an education that fails to place a heavy emphasis on the humanities is a missed opportunity. Without a base in humanities, both the students—and the democratic society these students must enter as informed citizens—are denied a full view of the heritage and critical habits of mind that make civilization worth the effort. . . . For those who go to college, the four years spent there are often the sole chance we give ourselves to think deeply and broadly about our place in the world. To turn college into nothing more than job training (emphasizing only those jobs that pay well), represents another missed opportunity for students and the society that needs them.[14]

Arts and humanities help us look to the past to create an informed future. Consider the aims of the University of Kentucky's School of Art and Visual Studies, whose faculty require students to take existing knowledge and "to create new things, to produce new ideas, to learn to look at the world in new ways, and to think critically about what they and others have done within their respective fields of discovery. Our students must learn to take criticism, to see what they have done as others see it, and to respond creatively. Students must learn to push past what they already know, do, and think, to seek within themselves new creative and intellectual frontiers."[15] Adaptability and progressive thinking fuel growth. Consider the example of a stagnant pond, which absorbs sunlight and nutrients but whose water does not move to new outlets. If STEM training, which is beneficial and necessary for America, takes place in isolation and churns in its own circle, stagnation can occur. Scientists possess the creativity and mindset to direct their knowledge into new channels and provide innovative breakthroughs. Like Kentucky's commissioner of the Department for Environmental Protection, educators may also ask, "What are we doing to be prepared?"[16] How do educators and leaders prepare this generation for a dynamic world? To answer the question, we must first understand and distinguish between the various voices and data points.

Contemporary Hostility

In 2014, President Obama commented, "A lot of young people no longer see the trades and skilled manufacturing as a viable career. But I promise you, folks can make a lot more, potentially, with skilled manufacturing or the trades than they might with an art history degree." Although the president insisted that there is "nothing wrong with an art history degree—I love art history," the sentiments expressed reflect a growing sentiment that studying the humanities is akin to a vow of personal poverty or, worse, a recipe for economic sclerosis.[17] Recently, Kentucky governor Matt Bevin stated bluntly, "All the people in the world that want to study French literature can do so, they are just not going to be subsidized by the taxpayer." He told reporters, "There will be more incentives to electrical engineers than French literature majors. There just will."[18] Meanwhile, on a visit to Eastern Kentucky University, Kentucky's lieutenant governor, Jenean Hampton, counseled students who hope to land a job after college, "I would not be studying history."[19] During the GOP primary debates, Florida senator Marco Rubio added laconically, "We need more welders and less philosophers."[20] We admit that society must make more space for vocational training. These statements, though hyperbolic, represent genuine perceptions.

They represent a current belief that public universities have bloated humanities departments. The data, however, tell a different story. The humanities are actually quite small. The American Academy of Arts and Sciences reports, "As a percentage of all bachelor's degrees, the core disciplines in the humanities disciplines fell in 2014 to their lowest recorded level, 6.1 percent, in all years going back to 1948, the period for which the academy has reliable numbers. As recently as the early 1990s (well after STEM fields were open to women and many preprofessional programs grew), the equivalent figure was 8 percent. The highest level ever was 17.2 percent in 1967."[21] Harvard, a place where one would guess postgraduation job prospects for all majors are quite high, reported a near 16 percent dip in the percentage of humanities majors (including history) within the student body. "The biggest problem, frankly," says Professor Scott Sprenger, "is the contradiction between the idea that college is career prep and the perception—or misperception—that the humanities have no role to play in that."[22] A statement by Vinod Khosla, cofounder of Sun Microsystems, echoes this sentiment: "More and more fields are becoming very quantitative, and it's becoming harder and harder to go from majoring in English or history to having optionality on various future careers and being an intelligent citizen in a democracy."[23]

It is natural for students to associate career preparation with a specific college major. "And," as Sprenger observes, "students often pick their major by the name of the profession embedded in the major's name—education: educator; accounting: accountant; nursing: nurse."[24] However, there is rarely such a direct correlation between major and career in the humanities or in today's dynamic economy. Philosophy graduates typically don't pursue careers as professional philosophers. Few English literature majors go on to make their career writing literature. Statistics show that, in fact, most end up involved in business in some form.

In the humanities, the link between the name of the major and practical career preparation is not immediately discernible. And many schools are addressing this cloudiness by offering hybrid paths. Eastern Kentucky University, for example, weds liberal arts with technical skills. Graduates in history buttress their job prospects by choosing from among twenty-three career paths designed to meld a broad liberal arts background with fields such as electronic media, journalism, public relations, advertising, paralegal sciences, geography, communication studies, management, and globalization and international affairs, among others.[25]

In another example, Wake Forest University established a program that helps students translate their marketable skills developed in humanities to a career upon graduation. The college's Innovation, Creativity and Entrepreneurship program, housed in the School of Business, offers an interdisciplinary minor in Entrepreneurship and Social Enterprise. The program provides core courses and electives in the various liberal arts divisions, and the concept of the minor is simple: coupled with any major within the college or the School of Business, it is designed to "enable students to enhance their skills in innovative, creative and entrepreneurial thought and action as applied to their specific discipline or career area of interest."[26]

Another major university characterizes its aim to illuminate the path to careers for its humanities graduates as follows: "For students wishing to land a job right after the BA degree, it is crucial to have a plan for developing a skillset that will be identifiable and attractive to employers."[27] But even humanities graduates do not always grasp the career potential of their studies. Take, for example, former Massachusetts governor Mitt Romney's tongue-in-cheek comment about his own major, English: "As an English major I can say this . . . as an English major your options are uh, you better go to graduate school, all right? And find a job from there."[28] Another prominent venture capitalist quipped that English graduates "end up working in a shoe store."[29]

Of course, some humanities majors—like Mitt Romney—run for president. And indeed, others actually do end up writing blockbuster fiction. J. K. Rowling majored in French and classics, and Stephenie Meyer majored in English literature. Jamie Dimon, CEO of JPMorgan Chase, majored in psychology; Ronald Reagan, fortieth president of the United States, majored in sociology; Samuel Palmisano, former CEO of IBM, studied history; and Carl Icahn, billionaire Wall Street mogul, graduated in philosophy.

To be sure, not every art history major will run a Fortune 500 company or write blockbuster fiction. And difficult economic times most certainly demand training that can result in immediate employment. Admittedly, many humanities success stories receive subsequent graduate and technical training. However, as more and more jobs become automated with advanced technologies, training in the liberal arts joined with technical skills will be rewarded in the marketplace.

As computers become more sophisticated, one commentator writes, "It is precisely the emotive traits that are rewarded: the voracious lust for understanding, the enthusiasm for work, the ability to grasp the gist, the empathetic sensitivity to what will attract attention and linger in the mind."[30] No training cultivates these so-called emotive traits better than the humanities.

MIT professors Erik Brynjolfsson and Andrew McAfee explain in their book *The Second Machine Age*[31] that while computers can now beat humans in games like chess and *Jeopardy!*, when humans work with a computer, the two together are stronger than either one alone. What humans add is just that, their humanity. This ever-strengthening link between technology and humans, or what Steve Jobs's biographer Walter Isaacson calls a "human-technology symbiosis," is what employers seem to crave and an agile democracy demands. Those who hire understand that "in a changing world, the question is no longer merely technical subjects vs. the humanities. Instead, students must understand that the world they are emerging into is rife with new challenges. Addressing those issues will require understanding both the pervasive technological and scientific foundation of our society, as well as the human beings who populate it."[32] Finding those with the social and communications skills cultivated in the humanities is a priority for employers.

Humanities' Role in the Workforce

Philip D. Gardner and his colleagues at the Collegiate Employment Research Institute, a research group housed at Michigan State University, regularly survey thousands of employers across sectors to determine hiring trends for college graduates. Gardner's surveys reveal that a substantial majority of employers look for the "best" candidate rather than a specific major. Meanwhile, hiring trends for humanities majors have seen an increase. According to recent reports, "Four categories showed double-digit increases: Arts, Humanities and Liberal Arts; Business; Communication and Media Studies; and Computer Science."[33]

In the past, Gardner summarized his findings this way: there are "only two choices" for college students who want to expand their options, that is, "to be a technically savvy liberal arts graduate or a liberally educated technical graduate."[34]

Critical thinking and writing are standard learning outcomes for universities. A study conducted by researchers at the Council for Aid to Education and New York University showed that these skills were significantly more developed by students who chose humanities, science, and engineering degrees than by those in business and education. Indeed, upon graduation not only were liberal arts and science majors more skilled in critical thinking and writing, but their relative improvement in those penetrating abilities since they entered college was also greater.[35]

Feedback from the president of a financial services company with more than twelve thousand employees confirms that skills acquired in a liberal education contribute to a desirable workforce:

> Business leaders today are looking for a diversity of skills, and not just technical knowledge. Pivotal right now in financial services—a relationship business—is trust built around empathy, understanding, listening skills, critical thinking. It's not enough in financial services to simply be able to work with a spreadsheet. You need to convince your individual or institutional clients to take the right set of actions. The skills that come out of the humanities, the softer relationship skills—listening, empathy, an appreciation for context—are incredibly important. Of the individuals in my organization who receive the most consistently positive feedback—who are most valued by our clients—only a sliver ever went to business school. Most of them learned their financial activities at our firm, but came into the firm with a much broader range of skills.[36]

Business majors are not alone in needing a healthy dose of humanities. Technology programmers benefit from the exposure to music or art. A former programmer, recounting complex coding problems that were solved by graduates in music and philosophy, observed, "I've worked in software for years and, time and again, I've seen someone apply the arts to solve a problem of systems. The reason for this is simple. As a practice, software development is far more creative than algorithmic." He further argues that humanities shouldn't be an afterthought, explaining that a trade like coding, while certainly not easy, may be learned through self-study, whereas "to enter the mind of an artist, you need a human guide."[37]

Learning subjects such as computer science and chemistry already takes time and mental energy; the prospect of adding, on top of this, mounds of reading in philosophical texts may seem daunting, impractical, or simply undesirable as it cuts into time used for employment or socializing. A student's existing economic situation is a hurdle to justifying liberal arts or a liberal education. In this sense, the liberal arts may appear to be reserved for the elite with the means to afford it.

But employability may demand it. The depth gained through humanities and a liberal education shouldn't be an either-or proposition with preparation for employment. Policy makers, administrators, and students must consider

(1) how humanities can bridge to immediate employment and (2) how humanities can enhance technical training.

The humanities are important for the depth and empathy they add to our lives. But, with employer feedback that increasingly suggests that a broad-based education and engagement with the humanities will also aid students in their immediate and future employment, perhaps the cost of not liberally educating a populace should be the real fear, especially as the humanities increase social understanding and play a critical role within America's economy and democracy.

SIX

Dynamic Challenges and Solutions in Higher Education

Multicolor threads bob to a cacophony of clicks and clacks as nimble hands guide a traditional loom to produce tightly woven fabrics. In nineteenth-century Japan, inventor Sakichi Toyoda observed this manual-powered ritual as his family used looms to produce colorful kimonos. The arduous labor, however, was frustrating. Fragile threads on looms frequently snapped. One broken thread created a run in the fabric that might go unnoticed until long into the process—wasting time and material and greatly frustrating the worker.

Toyoda's Story and Seeds of Higher Education Solutions

Toyoda saw this "heartbreaking predicament" over and over, explains Professor Steven Spear in his book *Chasing the Rabbit*. "To solve this problem," he writes, "Toyoda committed himself to inventing a loom that would automatically stop the moment a strand broke. He dubbed the idea that work should stop when and where a problem occurred *Jidoka* (which was translated into English as autonomation, meaning 'self-regulation')."[1] Toyoda, who has been hailed as the Thomas Edison of Japan, produced numerous innovations to the loom.[2] Yet, his concept of Jidoka proved relevant well beyond the textile industry. Toyoda Loom Works expanded during World War I and, under the direction of Toyoda's son Kiichiro, the family swapped out their "d" for a "t" and started producing automobiles. Over the next century, Toyota evolved into one of the greatest twentieth-century triumphs of the automotive industry. Jidoka—as we will see—played a vital role in Toyota's success, and as we explore, might also play a role in addressing the difficulties facing higher education.

The Challenges Facing Higher Education

Higher education faces challenges. According to journalist Goldie Blumenstyk: "Skepticism regarding higher education's value is on the rise as the cost of college soars higher than most other services. Student debt is estimated at more than $1 trillion, and some indicators suggest that colleges may in fact be exacerbating economic inequality it aims to combat. Meanwhile, consumers are pushing higher education to adopt more efficient modes of delivery and coursework that will lead directly to jobs and careers upon graduation."[3]

In addition, the federal student loan program—which was developed to expand access to education—may contribute to tuition hikes. And meanwhile, the state's contributions to higher education are shrinking at a time when they may be the most vital funding source worth preserving and improving. Before further delving into the ways in which college provides returns to the Commonwealth—we have addressed them in prior chapters—here we focus on the challenges that face higher education. We also detail potential frameworks for finding solutions to these problems.

College Students Are Not Learning Enough

In 2011, Richard Arum and Josipa Roksa published perhaps the most-cited book in the contemporary debate surrounding higher education. The aptly titled *Academically Adrift* shook the assumption that students are learning at college.[4] The book analyzes test results from some 2,300 college-age students in a variety of four-year postsecondary colleges and universities who took the Collegiate Learning Assessment (CLA)—a test designed to gauge gains in analytical abilities and critical thinking. Results of the test found that 36 percent of college students "did not demonstrate any significant improvement in learning"[5] after four years of postsecondary schooling. And during the first two years of college this percentage includes almost half of all students. And, for those who did show improvement, gains were modest.

> More troubling still, the limited learning we [Arum and Roksa] have observed in terms of the absence of growth in CLA performance is largely consistent with the accounts of many students, who report that they spend increasing numbers of hours on nonacademic activities, including working, rather than on studying. They enroll in courses that do not require substantial reading or writing assignments; they interact with their professors outside of classrooms rarely, if ever; and they define and understand their college experiences as being focused more on social than on academic development.[6]

Arum and Roksa's findings are discouraging, but, as commentators point out, they do not prove a lack of growth in other arenas aside from CLA performance. The study analyzes, for example, critical thinking broadly rather than identifying specific disciplinary gains. Roksa and Arum acknowledge as much, stating, "A generic measure of critical thinking, complex reasoning, and writing did not do justice to what faculty within disciplines were working to develop in their students."[7]

Nonetheless, for Arum and Roksa the culprit is a lack of "rigor," especially extensive collegiate reading and writing. Activities that take time away from independent study—clubs, fraternities, and even group study—they conclude, diminish a student's likelihood of effective learning. "Educational practices associated with academic rigor improved student performance," they write, "while collegiate experiences associated with social engagement did not."[8] Of course, as we discussed earlier in the book, such activities develop communication and leadership skills that may complement and harness critical thinking and complex reasoning. Arum and Roksa's aim is not to eliminate socializing; they merely want students and educators to understand the trade-offs. Colleges can do a better job of inculcating discipline and rigor to counter the natural tendency, for some college-aged students, to focus on their social life on campus instead of their studies or even basic current events. Arum appropriately asks, "How do you sustain a democratic society when large numbers of the most educationally elite sector of your population are not seeing it as a normal part of their everyday experience to keep up with the world around them? We need higher education to take the institutional responsibility for educating people broadly to see [awareness] as a basic part of civic life."[9]

The issue is exacerbated by the need of many students—to mitigate student loans or support families—to balance their time in school with full-time work. According to Arum and Roksa, students on average spend only about twelve hours per week studying; much of the rest of their time is split between work, class, and social activities.[10] While more time needs to be dedicated to study, this negotiation of a balance between work, school, and social life is in many ways vital preparation for life beyond the campus. Later, we discuss the successes of work-study schools. Students certainly need more time to cultivate the critical thinking and reasoning skills essential for the knowledge-based economy; but they also need opportunities to grow in ways that often do not translate well on standardized tests.

While it's not always possible for colleges to nudge students to study, instructors at least have a somewhat captive audience in the classroom. To use the classroom to its fullest capacity, the university must help lecturers sharpen their skills. Teaching assistants, tutors, and writing coaches may be provided to supplement classroom learning. Ultimately, however, students must take the initiative, even as, in the classroom and throughout the campus community, universities can do better to foster an academic climate in which critical think-ing is cultivated and students receive the training they are paying to receive.

We add our call for learning to be the central goal of universities, and we acknowledge that many modern distractions, both on and off campus, can detract from that aim. Nationally, many universities and students are failing to invest in sufficiently rigorous academic activity, whether due to competing demands on their time, failure to prioritize learning, or a need for universities to offer more rigor.

Research Institutions May Lack Teaching Orientation

Another challenge for universities is to balance the focus on research and teaching. If the goal of higher education is learning, a critical input is teaching. Aspects of the tenure system in some institutions may reward subject matter mastery and production of novel information far more than the transmission of that information to the uninitiated student. As mentioned earlier, this has led politicians and other stakeholders to increasingly scrutinize the system.

Tenure promotes academic freedom and rewards scholars who have spent years devoted to subject mastery. It helps incentivize individuals to pursue ac-ademic research and to promote civic advancement through discovery and scholarship. But the standard research-based tenure process is not always fo-cused primarily on student learning outcomes. The solution is not to eliminate tenure but to ensure that instruction is excellent, student learning is high, and that there is access to remedial assistance where necessary.

Commentator Naomi Schaefer Riley has argued that effective teaching can be measured and, in turn, rewarded: "Good teaching involves preparation for lectures and discussions, extensive work in grading and a lot of contact with students. Those are all elements that students as well as faculty colleagues and school administrators could recognize and reward if they chose to." She continues, "The best way to improve the quality of education for college stu-dents is to get professors to focus more on teaching. And to do that we need to ditch the tenure system and start evaluating professors on the basis of their teaching ability, without any guarantee that they will keep their jobs if they don't continue to measure up over the years."[11]

To be clear, we believe research-related tenure has immense value to a democratic society. However, it is also true that it is difficult for universities to properly balance the competing priorities of research and teaching students. After assessing the modern system, several scholars have observed, "Although we state publicly that we want to create educational environments that con-tribute to better outcomes for students, we do not reward faculty in ways that promote these better outcomes. The tenure process favors increased research rather than improved teaching, and this calls for reconsideration so all priorities can be met. Specifically, out-of-class contact does not appear to be rewarded in higher education institutions."[12] Focused advancement of knowledge should not come at the expense of its effective dissemination, and vice versa.

Learning May Not Translate to Work Skills

For many, higher education's value lies in the dividends it pays to the student through employment. According to a study published in 2015, fewer than 30 percent of employers believe that graduates possess the skills required for success in the workforce.[13] A March 2016 report by American Public Media's *Marketplace* and the *Chronicle of Higher Education* determined, "When it comes to the skills most needed by employers, job candidates are lacking most in written and oral communication skills, adaptability and managing multiple priorities, and making decisions and problem solving."[14] While more than nine of ten employers consider critical thinking and writing to be "very important" for success on the job, 60 percent of managers felt that 2016 graduates lacked critical thinking skills and 44 percent of managers felt they lacked writing skills.[15] Furthermore, employers note that only 16 percent of graduates achieve excellence in written communication and only 28 percent achieve excellence in critical thinking.[16] These findings are consistent with Arum and Roksa's study that measures growth in critical thinking skills during college. They found that those students who scored low "are more likely to be living at home with their parents, burdened by credit-card debt, unmarried, and unemployed."[17]

Kevin Carey notes that key players in higher education probably don't relate well to those who graduated from college and are still not equipped to succeed. According to Carey, employment is achieved disproportionately by the privileged who "matriculate well prepared for college. They are given challenging work to do and respond by learning a substantial amount in four years. Other students graduate from mediocre or bad high schools and enroll in less-selective colleges that don't challenge them academically. They learn little. Some graduate anyway, if they're able to manage the bureaucratic necessities of earning a degree."[18] In this way, some argue, college is merely about sorting.

At its worst, college becomes a system where each entity works in isolation rather than in concert: students enjoy the social experiences they want, professors pursue their academic interests, administrators bolster the institution's finances and reputation, and the government advances scientific discovery. Sadly, according to Arum and Roksa, "No actors in the system are primarily interested in undergraduate student academic growth, although many are interested in student retention and persistence. Limited learning on college campuses is not a crisis because the institutional actors implicated in the system are receiving the organizational outcomes that they seek, and therefore neither the institutions themselves nor the system as a whole is in any way challenged or threatened."[19] For all the time, money, and mental energy put into a college education, stakeholders—especially employers—expect to see returns on investments through valuable participation in the economy. But the gap between employer needs and college production can be disconcerting.[20]

College Education Does Not Guarantee Employment

A college education does not always translate into a job, especially for the large group of students who do not develop employable skills, including complex reasoning, critical thinking, the habit of hard work, and communication abilities. In the past several years the trend has been improving as the economy has experienced some sustained growth. In 2018, for those over twenty-five years old who have a college degree, the unemployment rate has hovered around 2.2 percent. However, the prospects are not always rosy. Young college graduates in 2014, for example, experienced 8.5 percent unemployment, up from 5.5 percent in 2007. And, according to the Economic Policy Institute, among college graduates who were employed in 2012, 44 percent were in a job that did not require a college degree. Yet the prospects were far worse for young workers without college degrees—in 2014, they experienced an astounding 22.9 percent unemployment.[21] Investment in an individual's education would ideally be capitalized upon by the student and prospective employers. But when the college degree does not represent the ability to add economic value, employment is not guaranteed.

Tuition Continues to Increase

Funding for a student's education comes from the individual student, the family, loans, and government subsidies or other potential sources such as endowment funds and outside scholarships. And while a higher tuition may seem to promise a premium learning experience, the money does not always—or even primarily—go toward teaching and learning experiences. Recent increases in tuition are caused by myriad factors. In addition to diminished state funding and changes to the federal loan system, other factors include compliance and safety costs, athletics, paraprofessionals, and various student-oriented counseling, activities, and advisement services. Whatever the specific causes, rising tuition can price low-income citizens out of higher education and further widen the income and education gaps; or it can financially burden those who pay for an education through loans. Additionally, as universities and regulations become increasingly intertwined, navigation of the web of rules and other student needs can siphon money to administrative departments; this protects professors' time from administrative tasks, but it also sometimes redirects funds from learning. The ballooning costs of bureaucracy and nonacademic services can contribute to the jaw-dropping tuition bills that students, families, and governments today are expected to pay. The numbers are sobering.

During the same period (1983 to 2012) in which the median family income increased 15.6 percent, the cost of tuition, fees, and room and board at public universities increased 129.1 percent.[22] But increased tuition has not always translated into a similar increase in learning. In 1975, there were two nonacademic staff for every 100 students; in 2005, five nonacademic staff served the same number of students.[23] Commentators recognize that part of this is the cost of expanding education to a wider range of Americans; but, for the average student, the tuition increases simply do not seem fair. There are almost twice the number of administrators and nonacademic staff today as faculty.[24] An economist at Centre College in Kentucky, Robert Martin, observes that campuses are expanding due to additions of services "beyond teaching and research."[25]

The situation may, however, be exacerbated by the general decrease in state funding and involvement in universities. According to Thomas Mortensen with the Pell Institute for the Study of Opportunity in Higher Education, almost 60 percent of university revenue came from the state in the late 1980s.[26] Now state support makes up, on average, less than 30 percent of university revenue, a trend that it appears will continue.[27] When states decrease stable funding sources it catalyzes competition to seek student dollars. The school that can attract dollars from a student stays open. One way in which colleges have kept students coming is by offering an array of attractive experiences and services beyond the classroom. These services carry costs that are often paid by affluent enrollees or by student loan dollars.

Ironically, however, the availability of student loans often makes it feasible for universities to increase tuition without much fear of losing students. With access to federal dollars, students are able to make good on their tuition bills, but by taking on more debt. With that said, students with the highest loan burdens are those who choose expensive private schools, and, in fact, debt levels for public colleges have remained relatively modest by comparison.

High tuition does more than weaken personal bank accounts; it further increases the income and education gaps between classes since universities seek students who can pay rather than individuals who might need the education the most. Policy analyst Stephen Burd admits, "Everybody wants the kids from the Northeast and California. They are wealthy and they tend to be good students."[28]

While the coasts may not be its primary recruiting ground, the University of Alabama has adopted a strategy to retain high academic achievers, as evidenced by its expenditure on merit-based aid, which is twice as high as what it pays for aid based on financial need. Burd observes that university efforts to vigorously recruit "the best prepared" and "most able to pay" leaves lower-income residents without affordable options. He says, "There is less aid for low-income students and there are fewer seats." About 27 percent of the state of Alabama's population is black, but only 11 percent of University of Alabama students are black, down from 15 percent in 2000.[29]

Students and universities may consider such high costs justifiable because the value of education is priceless. But the trajectory in price increases is not healthy for democracy, equality, or economic mobility; it leaves out a large portion of the American populace who cannot afford the experience.

Experimentalist Approach

A lot of serious issues face higher education. We have listed only a few. Not all universities are cut from the same cloth, and solutions to these problems must be tailored to specific institutions. The challenges facing a public flagship are different than those facing a private liberal arts school. The issues confronting a four-year vocational-oriented college differ from those at a research-intensive institution. And some issues that we have not mentioned—such as campus safety, diversity, college athletics, or sexual assault—merit much longer treatments.

While some have floated proposals for sweeping, across-the-board changes to higher education in the United States, it is likely that concrete solutions to most of the problems will be tackled on individual campuses through the collective efforts of faculty, staff, administrators, students, alumni, and their surrounding campus communities.

We will not try to offer sound-bite solutions. Rather we suggest heuristics to enable individual institutions to solve, or at least address, these problems at the local level. Drawing on scholarly work on experimentalist government, led by Columbia's Charles Sabel, we detail how certain principles of innovation and experimentation might apply in governing the academy. In recent years, a small cadre of academics and social scientists has taken heart from organizational successes that have popped up in disparate arenas. While the problems are diverse, the principles behind their solutions are similar.

Rather than posit perfect planning and execution (which many models of higher education hierarchies tend to emphasize), these experimentalist systems—like the Toyota model mentioned at the outset of this chapter—assume imperfect policies and then plan accordingly. These experimentalist systems are built to test, learn, and improve by rooting out flaws early, finding unexpected solutions, and broadcasting those solutions as widely as possible. In this model, those who find problems are promoted—not punished. By expecting flaws, these systems actually grow much closer to operational perfection than their traditional bureaucratic and hierarchical siblings. This experimentalist approach to problem solving is vividly illustrated in Toyota's story and, as we explore, is increasingly applied with promising results throughout the public sector, including higher education.

Before we explore Toyota's dynamic, self-regulating approach—alluded to earlier—let's consider Ford Motor Company's original mass production and assembly-line approach. Henry Ford streamlined the car-making process by dividing labor into dozens of phases. Workers were trained to do one step, and parts were delivered to workers. As workers mastered their roles, production speed increased. The Model T factory reached unprecedented levels of productivity. In ten years the company produced ten million cars. It was, at the time, the apogee of mass production and the envy of the world. While others would modify the system, its most salient elements are still present in modern mass assembly lines. And yet, despite its success in efficiencies through scale, the traditional assembly line had flaws. Those same top-down linear flaws are present in many bureaucratic institutions, including colleges and universities. It took an upstart automobile manufacturer in Japan to root them out.

Principles from Toyota

Costs of Inflexibility and Need for Customization

With time it became evident that mass production faced systemic problems. Though increases in production speed appeared to reduce overall costs, sometimes assembly lines increased speed while masking costly problems. In many assembly lines, anyone perceived as slowing things down—even for valid safety reasons—was persona non grata. If you drew too much attention by pointing out problems, you could find yourself out of work. For many line managers, acknowledging problems simply slowed production, and, thus, workers were often unintentionally incentivized to create workarounds to artificially boost speed and, in some cases, hide problems and production flaws. Managers encouraged such behavior by trying to meet production quotas at all costs.

As a result, systemic problems with parts and machines went underreported. Stockpiling parts became the norm. If a defective part came down the line, swapping it out was faster than halting production to discover and fix the underlying issue. This, of course, had deleterious long-term effects—machines went unfixed and reoccurring problems went uninvestigated. Furthermore, stockpiling led to disorderly factories and significant long-term productivity losses. There were also larger issues related to supply and demand. Increased productivity was only desirable when demand was high. When supply outpaced demand, mass production could quickly become a liability.

Jidoka, or self-regulation, in the textile industry meant that when a string broke, the loom stopped. In automobile manufacturing, when a problem arose on the Toyota assembly line, workers and machines would immediately stop. The problem was flagged and fixed. Rather than slow down production, as some would presume, the long-term result was actually a drastic increase in production and a reduction in long-term costs and waste. Jidoka also came to include control of supply and demand, as Toyota implemented the just-in-time pull method.

Toyota legend Taiichi Ohno is credited with helping overcome identified flaws in mass production by his design and implementation of the just-in-time method. This helped address the mass production problem of pairing supply and demand. As Steven Spear explains, "Ohno developed a simple rule to make sure that the pieces acted together in a self-regulating synchronization: If someone—the 'customer'—needed something, he had to go ask for it, and the 'supplier' was not allowed to produce and deliver something until asked." The idea was to keep upstream actions aligned with downstream requests so that there was no superfluous stockpiling or lag times. "Needs downstream pace work upstream so individual work is *in service to the larger process and ultimately are linked in service to the end customer, none acting in isolation.*"[30] These core innovations had the added effect of producing two additional (often overlooked) beneficial practices. The first was a robust and rapid response to system failures, which led to lasting fixes and institutional learning, and the second was institutionalized communication among machines, line workers, and management, which continually spread information on problems, fixes, and best practices.[31] Efficiency increased.

To fully grasp how the Toyota Production System differed from traditional mass production, it is helpful to walk through the manufacturing steps from beginning to end. It might begin with a customer's request for a Camry. The factory then kicks into gear. The workers only request the parts they need for the one Camry (nothing is wasted). The process continues until shipment and delivery. If a problem occurs to a part or machine, the issue is flagged by workers (or, more likely today, software). Once the flaw is flagged, the whole process immediately stops. Assembly workers, along with technicians and managers, begin the process of discerning what went wrong. Because the source of the problem may be several steps downstream (and associated with a particular machine) the group asks "why" at least five times until they get to the root cause—the problem that caused the dominos to fall. Once the flaw is ascertained, the facility's experts implement a permanent fix. There are no workarounds and no messy stockpiles.[32]

Transparency and Problem Targeting

Through this process, the factory disseminates beneficial information regarding how to fix the issue. Managers, assembly line workers, and technicians are all informed about the defect, why it occurred and how to fix it (or avoid it in the future).[33] Only after the investigation runs its course and the fix is implemented does production proceed. The results from Toyota's performance over the past half-century speak for themselves.[34] Even with recent setbacks (including the economic downturn, large-scale recalls, and an 18.5 percent slide in profits after the 2010 Japanese tsunami), Toyota has consistently outpaced international competition and their practices have become industry standard.[35] Today, the Toyota Production System or "lean manufacturing" is used by some of the world's top manufacturers, including Apple.

Continued Self-Regulation, Evaluation, Improvement

Any corporation can master superior manufacturing techniques, but if it does not have great products or does not continually improve and reinvent those products it will not succeed in the way Toyota so clearly has—that's where *kaizen* comes in. "Kaizen" is a Japanese word meaning "continuous improvement," and it serves as Toyota's unofficial mantra. While kaizen certainly applies to their continuous improvement techniques in manufacturing, it also applies to their R&D operation, where they have overcome gaps and entered new markets by creating successful lines to appeal to youth (Scion), use less fossil fuels (Prius), and offer competitive luxury (Lexus). Thus, the Toyota Production System was a dual technique: a superior manufacturing system (the just-in-time model, Jidoka, and information dissemination) and a never-ending pursuit to improve and innovate.

Experimentalism Applied in Government Settings

How does all of this apply to higher education? All kinds of hierarchies suffer from flaws similar to those found in mass production. First, there is often a disconnect between the facts on the ground and the original plan. Second, channels typically are not in place to provide feedback from the circumstances on the ground. Third, employees are often not incentivized to try to reform the system but are incentivized to seek workarounds so as not to ruffle administrative feathers. Workarounds, while initially attractive, and sometimes rewarded by mid-level bosses, often undermine or cause unforeseen problems in a master plan put forward by top administrators designing the systems.

Toyota, even with top-down managerial structures and complex plans, assumes that their blueprints are flawed from the start and will continually require refinement when actually implemented. They further assume that many flaws will yet be discovered. This does not mean that their original plans are sloppy. Quite the contrary—Toyota strives to get the plan as perfect as possible before implementation—but they wisely design the system in anticipation of finding many imperfections. Whereas traditional hierarchical bureaucracies—especially in government—rarely assume that flaws will emerge when implementing plans and strive to minimize any deviation from their original plans (until, perhaps, a crisis arises), Toyota knows changes will occur so they embed systems into the master plan that are meant to discover flaws and then respond quickly to fix them. Each solution is then shared broadly.

This model stands in stark contrast to traditional hierarchical bureaucracies, government or otherwise. In such systems, just as in mass production, serious flaws may go unreported, or, sometimes, may be intentionally hidden for years.

VHA: Failure in Traditional Hierarchical Bureaucracies

The Veterans Health Administration (VHA), part of the US Department of Veterans Affairs, provides laudatory health care and medical services for military veterans in hospitals throughout the United States. Like many government-run systems, however, the VHA has in the past operated on a command and control philosophy reflective of hierarchical bureaucracies generally, with systems that are developed and specific guidelines and goals that are set by those in command—agency employees or federal lawmakers. In recent years, when the implementation of the guidelines or goals did not pan out in reality, some managers and employees resorted to workarounds (the equivalent of stockpiling in manufacturing). Stockpiles allow production to continue even if there are systemic problems in need of fixing somewhere along the line. In the case of the VHA scandal during the Obama presidency, employees had resorted to keeping two sets of lists, one of the actual hospital statistics and a second list that they sent to the administration—which had false statistics that showed continual success. This is a classic workaround.

Hidden from managers was the fact that excessively long wait times were resulting in poor veteran treatment. At one Arizona hospital, some forty veterans died while they waited to be seen by a health care professional. Notes listing people as "deceased" were removed from reports. Such unflattering realities were hidden to make statistics look better than they really were. When whistle-blowers initially sought explanations, they only received retaliation. Eventually they went to the press. The culture was not one of Jidoka.

Experimentalism Applied in University Settings

There is a better way. The principles of Toyota's system have been applied to child welfare programs, public education, and numerous industries and nongovernmental organizations (NGOs), including major hospital systems and food kitchens. Even with these successful applications of the Toyota Production System, few commentators have looked at how they could be used to solve some of higher education's most vexing problems, including responding to the needs of students, employers, and society. Experimental systems are often put into place as a result of crises. As president of the University of California Janet Napolitano notes, "If every crisis presents an opportunity, then the opportunity is now to ensure that higher education remains a distinguishing feature in the fabric of our republic."[36]

Without realizing it, Toyota challenged and ultimately rewrote the foundational assumptions of mass production. Toyota applied the principle of self-regulation or self-evaluation by assuming future problems and creating processes to address them. It pursued flawlessness by thorough examination of problems and resolution of setbacks before moving forward. The company remained flexible, lean, and customizable—creating cars one order at a time. And Toyota was internally transparent; it did not hide problems internally but made them widely known so solutions could be garnered from all collaborators. Universities would strengthen their offerings to the American public by adoption of these principles of responsiveness, flexibility, customization, and continuous improvement.

Some institutions of higher education already embrace experimental changes. One way to increase revenues and improve job prospects would be to increase graduation rates at two-year and four-year colleges without compromising academic standards and learning outcomes. There are significant costs in recruiting, admitting, orienting, housing, and, finally, teaching students. If a student decides to drop out, the school loses future tuition payments and may, in the end, have spent more on a student (and services to that student) than it received through tuition. Though universities are not about profits, and educating an individual is vastly different than making a car, the current models for increasing graduation rates are not too far off from the principles at work in the Toyota Production System. Society relies on universities to produce students with certain abilities; Toyota's customers expect high-quality products. The analogy is imperfect; universities are not production plants. However, similar principles are necessary for success in both arenas. Schools such as Ball State, Georgia State, and Southern New Hampshire University serve as examples, as these very different universities strive to implement new technology and intervention plans to help retain students while also trying to maintain high academic standards.

Ball State, Georgia State, and Big Data

David Letterman is perhaps Ball State University's most famous alumnus. And in 2000 when his alma mater's football team was enduring one of the longest losing streaks in NCAA history, Letterman intervened by having his guest, the famed Magic Johnson, deliver a pep talk for the team. It apparently worked. The team ended its twenty-one-game losing streak, beating Miami of Ohio.[37]

Today Ball State is experimenting with interventions of another kind. They take part in the University Innovation Alliance, a group of public universities backed by large foundations and charged with using "data analytics . . . aimed at improving graduation rates for needy students."[38]

As journalist Goldie Blumenstyk puts it, "Tools developed in-house and by a slew of companies now give administrators digital dashboards that can code students red or green to highlight who may be in academic trouble." If that weren't enough, "Handsome 'heat maps'—some powered by apps that update four times a day—can alert professors to students who may be cramming rather than keeping up," and "as part of a broader effort to measure the 'campus engagement' of its students, Ball State University in Indiana goes so far as to monitor whether students are swiping in with their ID cards to campus-sponsored parties at the student center on Saturday nights."[39]

Universities are doing this because studies show "that students who are more engaged with college life are also more likely to graduate." The same goes for students who are doing poorly in class. But now, armed with data that allow schools to pinpoint problems, schools can intervene. "When a student's card-swipe patterns suggest she's stopped showing up for clubs or socials, a retention specialist will follow up with a call or an email to see how she's doing." Blumenstyk continues: "Ball State is also tracking ID card swipes at the career center and student-leadership programs. It even put out a mobile app this fall [2014] for the 1,200 low-income freshmen who qualify for Pell Grants. The app rewards students with points based on the activities that the university monitors. They can redeem these points for merchandise at the campus bookstore. A quarter of eligible students are taking part."[40]

Of course, Ball State is not the first school to try its hand at using big data to address graduation rates. Georgia State University used ten years of data to devise "intervention initiatives," also "including a robust advising program, to help its students stay on track." For example, when students sign up for the wrong class or a class that will not help them graduate, they receive a call from retention specialists. These efforts resemble Toyota's method of stopping production and fixing any problem they see on the line. According to the numbers, Georgia State's intervention program appears to be working. "Although state funding has declined and the number of economically disadvantaged students has increased," according to a report from the *Atlanta Journal-Constitution*, "the college has seen a rise in its graduation rates for students who earned their degrees within six years, including those for minority students. Ten years ago, Georgia State's graduation rate hovered around 32 percent. It increased to almost 54 percent last year, approaching the national six-year rate of 59 percent reported by the National Center for Education Statistics."[41]

Southern New Hampshire: Retention of Students Online

The problems facing higher education are broader than graduation rates, and universities should look at using experimentalist government in a variety of contexts. Two schools are trying to do so in notable ways. Whereas Ball State and Georgia State are striving to improve graduation rates on campus, some schools are applying experimentalist principles to methods of delivering instruction, an innovation that may promise to save students money while extending universities' offerings well beyond the core campus. Unfortunately, so-called MOOCs or massive open online courses, offered by schools like MIT and Harvard, have failed to retain many students (only 5 percent of students who enroll in a class complete it).[42] Two of the most intriguing case studies of institutions striving to fix this problem come from unexpected locations: southeastern Idaho and Manchester, New Hampshire.

In 2001 Ricks College, a small, rural two-year junior college in Rexburg, Idaho, became a four-year university with an enrollment of 30,000 students from all across the United States and the globe. The name changed from Ricks College to Brigham Young University–Idaho. This shift from a two-year to a four-year school allowed administrators to design a university afresh.

The first two presidents who had the most influence in transforming the institution were former business school faculty members and administrators. BYU–Idaho's second president was long-time dean of the Harvard Business School, Kim Clark. Clark saw an opportunity in BYU–Idaho to innovate on an already student-focused model. "BYU-Idaho will continue to be teaching oriented," a press release stated at the time of the transition. "Effective teaching and advising will be the primary responsibilities of its faculty who are committed to academic excellence. The institution will emphasize undergraduate education and will award baccalaureate degrees; graduate degree programs will not be offered. Faculty rank will not be a part of the academic structure of the four-year institution. BYU-Idaho will operate on an expanded year-round basis, incorporating innovative calendaring and scheduling while also taking advantage of advancement in technology which will enable the four-year institution to serve more students."[43]

Such dramatic changes in a campus are not for every institution. But, considering that this announcement came in 2000, it seems remarkably prescient given how it faces some of the contemporary challenges now facing the academy. Clark would not take over until 2005, after the school had worked out many of its growing pains and accommodated thousands more students each year. The first challenge was to educate more than twenty-five thousand students on campus, with space for only fifteen thousand. Eventually the university came up with a system in which students enroll in two of three trimesters each year and are required to take at least one online course per semester.

Under the direction of Clark, the university once again sought to expand enrollment by launching an ambitious online education program. But administrators noted that students—especially those enrolled online—often failed to make it through the first year of classes.[44] So BYU–Idaho further refined the model with the "Pathway" program. In preparation for the rigors of either full-time matriculation or an online program, students met in a local group each week and took a student-led class (guided by volunteers who are retired professors, educators, or educated professionals called "facilitators").[45] The other classes taught online are basic college writing, introduction to algebra, and personal finance. As the program's website states, "Each semester during Pathway, students take a light course load consisting of both academic and religious education. Pathway courses are designed to help students learn basic skills and gain the confidence and abilities needed to succeed in college and in life."[46] While the academic courses are taken online, life skills and religion courses are delivered in person locally with Pathway facilitators.

Facilitators support students in their academic progress and help them work through the basic online courses. With efficient use of resources, including volunteer retirees who serve as facilitators, part-time professors as online instructors, and class meetings held in person at church meetinghouses free of overhead, tuition costs are almost incomparably low (about $65 per credit or $3,900 for associate degrees or $7,800 for bachelor's degrees).[47] Since the program is specifically designed to help those who would otherwise not seek out a college education to obtain a degree, certification, or at least some college training, the university expects low retention. But it also removes one of the largest barriers for student retention, high tuition. Through the Pathway program, students who have never attended college, or those who attended some college but never completed their degree and would like to finish, can pay for a college degree on a minimum wage salary.[48]

New Hampshire is known for its quaint New England villages, some of which look as though things haven't changed since colonial America. Few think of the "live free or die" state as a hotbed for innovation. Yet, nestled alongside the Merrimack River in the city of Manchester is Southern New Hampshire University. In 2012, *Fast Company Magazine* included SNHU as one of the most innovative organizations in America, alongside the likes of Apple and Google.[49]

When Paul LeBlanc took over the university, it was just a sleepy college with fewer than two thousand students. Today, thanks to online enrollment, it has tens of thousands of students across the United States and brings in $200 million in revenue. *Slate* magazine said, "It's the Amazon.com of higher education" with a "burgeoning online division [that] has 180 different programs with an enrollment of 34,000. Students are referred to as 'customers,'" and the university aims to undercut competitors on tuition. The school also "deploys data analytics for everything from anticipating future demand to figuring out which students are most likely to stumble. 'We are super-focused on customer service, which is a phrase that most universities can't even use,'"[50] says SNHU's LeBlanc.

The delivery of education at SNHU is very different than that on typical campuses. Most of the online instructors are adjunct and are paid only $2,000 to $3,000 per class. And rather than delivering the information based on their own learning and the class's individual needs, the instructors mostly facilitate the online delivery of standardized course modules—the information is stored online rather than in a professor's brain. And although instructors are there to assess (when applicable) and lead online class discussions, the "instructor's main job is to swoop in when a student is in trouble. Often, they don't pick up the warning signs themselves. Instead, SNHU's predictive analytics platform plays watchdog, sending up a red flag to an instructor when a student hasn't logged on recently or has spent too much time on an assignment."[51]

Through this system the school can intervene to help students reach their goal of completing a course and obtaining their degree. Ultimately, SNHU administrators believe this is in the best interest of the student who has already paid tuition. These and other models will not work for every school. But the process of innovation and the use of experimentalist problem solving can help administrations and faculty craft institution-specific solutions.

How Higher Education Could Improve Its Model

This chapter presents a few ways in which colleges are helping improve retention and graduation rates through using immediate intervention to prevent students from dropping out. This technique is similar to the Toyota model, in which a problem that arises in the assembly line triggers a pause in the system while workers find the cause, implement a fix, and then broadcast the solution so that factory workers and others readily know how to address the problem in the future, as they gradually and continually improve.

Once again, graduating college students is very different from manufacturing cars. For starters, the Toyota model mainly addresses the malfunction of machines, whereas college students are human beings with hearts and minds, not broken widgets. Students encounter challenges that impede their progress. Where appropriate, professors and administrators can intervene to teach, aid, empower, and encourage young people as they navigate their growing and learning experiences.

At Georgia State, administrators realized many students were dropping out of school because of financial shortcomings as low as $300. They implemented a micro-grant program to help struggling students stay in school while they found ways to cover their financial needs. Other fixes can be more complex. Students might drop out of college for a variety of emotional or other personal reasons. In an online setting, an institution may not do anything more than have the instructor remind a student of deadlines or coach a student through an assignment. This intervention, though important, would not necessarily treat the underlying issues that result in the student falling behind.

In the Toyota model, teams are assembled to help find solutions for an individual issue. These investigative groups are flexible. They draw conclusions but are attuned to changing circumstances to find the best solutions. In a college setting, such an approach could result in satisfactory long-term solutions for student underperformance or other pressing concerns. The decision to budget resources to assist struggling students (whether online or on campus) offers a more deliberate plan than intervention with retention representatives, who may offer only temporary fixes to profound difficulties. Many of our social programs function this way, treating symptoms rather than root causes. Education, however, intends to treat root causes early on in life.

We opened this chapter by scrutinizing traditional hierarchical bureau-

cracies—whether in government or universities. Yet more and more traditional organizations are rebuilding with "experimentalist" models that operate in
anticipation of bumps in the road. Experimentalists build systems that learn.
They actively discover problems and then implement fixes. Once the fix is discovered, they broadcast solutions widely through their institution. Meanwhile,
such institutions are constantly rethinking and even reinventing their models
to ensure that they remain relevant in an age of changing needs. The president
of Southern New Hampshire University said, "We want to create the business
model that blows up our current business model because if we don't, someone
else will."[52] This kind of experimentalism has defined America, and in order
to preserve some of the country's great institutions, visionary leaders need to
embrace this spirit in institution-specific doses; not every university needs to
blow up its model, but all should be eagerly seeking to improve, refine, and
retool to help students meet the demands of a dynamic world.

SEVEN

Higher Education at Work for the Commonwealth

In his inaugural address at Johns Hopkins University in 1876, Daniel Coit Gilman spoke about his vision for higher education generally and for his own institution specifically:[1]

> It is a reaching out for a better state of society than now exists; it is a dim but an indelible impression of the value of learning; it is a craving for intellectual and moral growth; it is a longing to interpret the laws of creation; it means a wish for less misery among the poor, less ignorance in schools, less bigotry in the temple, less suffering in the hospital, less fraud in business, less folly in politics; it means more study of nature, more love of art, more lessons from history, more security in property, more health in cities, more virtue in the country, more wisdom in legislation, more intelligence, more happiness, more religion.

The jury may still be out as to how institutions of higher education have done in each of these areas, but the 140-year-old charge is as relevant as when it was issued.[2]

Consider the word "university": the prefix, *uni,* Latin for "unity, to be one"; and the stem, *vers,* "to turn." Although disciplines on campus may be as diverse as professorial opinions, and backgrounds as divergent as areas of study, those in the academy should be committed to one united goal: the discovery, pursuit, transmission, and dissemination of knowledge. A literal brother- and sisterhood committed to truth binds scholars and students together across cultural, political, economic, and social boundaries. Among the sea of European languages, one word has emerged as a symbol of this scholarly unity: "university." At least in Latin, Dutch, Danish, French, German, Italian, Norwegian, Portuguese, Russian, Spanish, and Swedish, the prefix and the stem of the word "university" are largely the same. Only the grammatical endings differ among these eleven languages.[3]

We began this book with the image of Daniel Boone as he surveyed what was then part of the English colony of Virginia (later to become Kentucky in 1792); he marveled at its natural beauty and chronicled its abundant resources as he contemplated its boundless opportunity for himself, his family, and for future generations. What then, have subsequent populations done with the resources afforded them in Kentucky?

In this chapter we focus on several specific areas in which four of Kentucky's distinctive institutions—two private and two public—have demonstrated dogged determination and vision to provide opportunities for students and solutions to seemingly intractable problems. In terms of service to students, the public–private institutional divide is less important than a shared commitment to responsibly equip them to engage with the world. The first is Berea College and its unique work-study program, which enables students, 23 percent of whom come from "at-risk" or "distressed" Appalachian counties, to gain a liberal arts education without paying tuition through working part-time at the college during the length of their collegiate careers. The second is Centre College in Danville, Kentucky, which hosts the nation's most extensive study abroad program with its all-but-mandatory global experience normally undertaken by each student, about 50 percent of whom are native Kentuckians, during his or her junior year. The third is the University of Kentucky's community-oriented health services outreach program. The program is one of the most expansive in the country and is a nationally recognized leader, with its presence in each of Kentucky's 120 counties and its profound impact on health and human services throughout the Commonwealth. Two of every three University of Kentucky students are from the Commonwealth, and the university strategically "closes the loop" by training and placing doctors, nurses, physicians' assistants, and therapists throughout the state.[4] Fourth is the nationally ranked aviation program at Eastern Kentucky University, which endeavors to meet the ever-increasing need for pilots across the globe, a demand that, according to some estimates, may be approaching crisis levels as more than 750,000 will be required to meet the future demand in air travel.[5] Aviation is just one program that appeals to Eastern Kentucky University's student body, 86 percent of whom are in-state students, and it is emblematic of the populace's desire to expand the state's reach.[6] These initiatives are each as diverse as the institutions that undertake them, but each also speaks to a uniquely Kentucky quality of hard work and care for others. They collectively communicate a consistent desire to use higher education to address acute societal needs, to make a difference in communities across the Commonwealth and beyond.

Berea College Puts Students to Work

Berea College proudly awards every "enrolled student a no-tuition promise."[7] The school's "Tuition Promise" scholarship adds up to nearly a hundred thousand dollars over four years of study at an idyllic campus in Madison County, Kentucky. As the folks at Berea often say, the college provides "the best education money can't buy." Unlike so many students who graduate today with accumulated debt, the great majority of Berea grads leave college with little to no encumbrances.[8]

Founded in 1855 by abolitionist John Gregg Fee, Berea was unique from its outset, given its practice of admitting white and black students in a fully integrated curriculum. This pathbreaking policy made it the first nonsegregated college in the South and one of only a handful of higher education institutions to admit both males and females in mid-nineteenth-century America. The institution's unique character continues today, as shown in its strong track record for diversity on campus and its commitment to being a "work college."[9]

In this regard, however, Berea has close company in Appalachia. Alice Lloyd College, in Pippa Passes, Kentucky, similarly provides tuition-free admission for students from the college's service area, thereby addressing pressing needs both immediate and long-term as the institution produces graduates who are educated to lead and transform their local communities. Alice Lloyd's "Appalachian Leaders College Scholarship" directly engages with students from 108 counties across numerous states; it brings them to campus, puts them to work while they study, and sends them out with the vision and skills to lead.[10] The school's program is as much about creating an "earning experience" that helps pay bills as it is about creating a genuine "learning experience as well."[11] The program aims to blend the hallmarks of a liberal arts education with the demonstrable experience demanded by employers.

Just as at Berea College, Alice Lloyd began with a vision of service and sacrifice. The college's founder, Alice Spenser Geddes Lloyd, would accept "sacks of potatoes and turnips as tuition" when classes first began in 1923.[12] Students were put to work on campus to offset their expenses just as early.[13] The need that existed then—to educate those who needed it most—continues now: one quarter of the college's class of 2018 came "from families whose total income is lower than three thousand dollars a year."[14] The payoff, as one might expect, is unrivaled: more than 80 percent of Alice Lloyd graduates return to serve the surrounding counties in their chosen profession.[15]

So, what attracts students to schools that require work in exchange for an education? What can we learn from such students? And what lessons can we glean from those colleges? The students at the nation's work colleges, the *New Yorker* finds, are generally "ambitious yet deeply practical" with "an eye toward employment after graduation." Ninety-nine percent of Berea's students are eligible for a Pell Grant.[16] These students want to acquire practical skills; they appreciate not only the "free" education, and the immersive experience in the liberal arts, but also the formative on-the-job training they receive. Richard Sennett, author of such books as *The Craftsman,* provides a philosophical foundation for student labor, one that contradicts common misperceptions about labor as foreign or undesirable. "The American system," he says, "is 'geared up for a service economy, where the idea is that people are going to prosper by getting farther and farther away from the world of skilled craftsmanship.'"[17] University of Massachusetts–Lowell professor Robert Forrant acknowledges that students at elite universities almost stereotypically "see themselves as designers, divorced from the dirty work of making." Students in work colleges recognize, and value, the interrelationship of learning and labor, of curriculum and craft.

The colleges that make educational opportunity possible in exchange for student labor are relatively small and self-contained by design as well as, perhaps, demand. Each college receives its federal work college designation by virtue of "a supervised work program . . . integral to its curriculum and mission . . . [that requires] all students to perform at least five hours each week [ten hours at Berea] of on-campus work."[18] All promote their liberal arts curriculum and take educating "the whole student" to levels few other institutions strive toward. Without sacrificing instructional quality or time to earn a degree, both Berea and Alice Lloyd codify their expectations for students' physical contributions to the campus and integrate them into the overall educational experience and the ethos of the institution. The expectations include the following:

Berea College Workplace Expectations

Exhibit enthusiasm for learning
Act with integrity and caring
Value all people
Work as a team
Serve others
Encourage plain and sustainable living
Celebrate work well done.[19]

Alice Lloyd Student Work Handbook

The Student Work Program is designed to accomplish the following purposes:

Promote a sense of dignity through work.
Promote a sense of service to others.
Enrich the educational program through experiential learning opportunities.
Provide students with monetary means to help finance their educational expenses and help gain a sense of accomplishment.
Enhance students' career opportunities.[20]

Work colleges recognize the realities of their students' lived experiences. They respond to the needs of students as they matriculate and anticipate ways to connect graduates with meaningful employment, opportunities to contribute to their community, and a sense of loyalty to their alma mater.

John Fee founded both the town and the school of Berea on illustrious models: the town is named for the ancient Christian city recorded in the book of Acts, and the South's first college to admit all races and both genders was initially modeled on Ohio's Oberlin College, which was "anti-slavery, anti-caste, anti-rum, anti-sin." The expectation of student work was as selfless as it was self-serving; students would offset their educational expenses and, more importantly, students would experience a wisdom that ran counter to the prevailing structures of the 1850s South: "manual labor would be embraced as a dignified task, thereby destigmatizing the work performed by slaves." The progressive tendency that influenced the school's social mission shaped the educational philosophy: "Reformers like John Dewey championed progressive education, emphasizing learning through experience; the mandatory work programs at places like Berea took Dewey's pragmatic philosophies a step further by weaving experience into the fabric of both their curricula and their operations."[21]

A glance at the employment section of Berea College's website at any given moment reveals many of those opportunities. Jobs are advertised for public safety officers, housekeepers, and administrative assistants. There are positions in paintings, ceramics, Appalachian Studies, or Social Justice Studies.[22] Those positions are only a small fraction of the work opportunities at Berea because the college's Labor Program features more than 1,500 student jobs, on campus and through community partnerships such as Habitat for Humanity ReStore,

New Opportunity School for Women, Berea Community School, Consult-Webs.com, Inc. (online support for law firms), MACED (the Mountain Association for Community Economic Development), Peacecraft (a nonprofit, fair-trade shop near campus), Save the Children Federation, and Sustainable Berea.[23]

The Labor Program was instituted as "The Fourth Great Commitment of Berea College," establishing it as a guiding presence more lasting than a mission statement or strategic plan. The school's Fourth Great Commitment is "To provide for all students through the Labor Program experiences for learning and serving in the community and demonstrate that labor, mental and manual, has dignity as well as utility." The recognition of service as central to mental development, not just moral or physical, distinguishes the school's mission. Students add value to the campus community and the surrounding town; their work contributes to a legacy in which "the Christian values of human compassion, dignity, and equality are expressed and lived."[24] Simultaneously mindful to preserve an intentionally developed tradition and prepare students to meet the economic realities of twenty-first-century life, Berea College recognizes the far-reaching impact of character developed through working while learning. Berea's current president, Dr. Lyle Roelofs, says the college strives for each "student to be an effective communicator, to be good at working in teams, good at leading teams but good at working together with other folks, have a good level of critical-reasoning ability—ability to analyze information both quantitatively and with attention to nuance and meaning."[25] The Labor Program Office tries to create "opportunities for students to work in major related areas and to develop soft skills that future employers are looking for."[26] The Program's "Goals and Expected Outcomes" flag the soft skills to be gained, "accountability, teamwork, initiative, respect, and life-long learning," and connect them to students' academic identities, through work that is "competency based (rather than credit hour based)." Long-term, the gains to society are the meaningful social and economic contributions these once economically disadvantaged students end up making in communities across Kentucky and the nation.[27]

The economic contribution Berea's students and graduates make to the Appalachian mountain region complements the college's investment in students. The loop is closed, then, when those graduates demonstrate a financial commitment to the school and community. Famously, Berea College benefits from an endowment equal to the nation's highest profile elite universities. The school maintains that available funds are put to exceptionally good use. Their development website explains that 75 percent of the college budget is built upon endowment income, with 16 percent federal and state funds, and 9 percent "from loyal alumni and friends through the Berea Fund."[28] Taken together, the school provides ultra-supportive, even life-changing, Tuition Promise scholarships for every student, to pay for that "best education money can't buy."[29]

Promotion of the flexibility that the billion-dollar endowment gives, though, draws attention even from stakeholders who have only a tangential interest in the college. In 2016, Berea's administration joined the leaders of similar schools on Capitol Hill to testify before the US House of Representatives' Ways and Means Committee. Berea's administration described the school's mission, its student population, and the generosity the endowment makes possible. They acknowledged that, on average, 68 percent of the annual endowment spendable return was used to fund scholarships and student financial aid, which directly met the need of the average Berea student, whose income for a family of four was just over $27,000, and of the 60 percent of that year's entering class who had an Expected Family Contribution of $0. They promoted the school's 86.3 percent fall-to-fall retention rate for new freshmen, the sort of statistic commonly associated with elite institutions with high-income student populations and not with students who must balance their individual pursuit of higher education with the pressing economic hardships left behind at home.[30]

The high-profile testimony at the Capitol made national headlines, but this attention was not especially new. For years, the public has been asking "whether the wealthiest universities are doing enough for the public good to warrant their tax exemption, or simply hoarding money to serve an elite few." Berea remains unique, though. Parents fret over FAFSAs and grants and loans. Legislators look for new dollars anywhere they can find them. Everyone agrees that students need help.[31] And Berea College continues to do what it has done since it began, giving students who have the most to gain a nearly unparalleled educational and work experience, one which shapes lives and transforms communities. And once they can, students, with characters shaped by doing good, give back. For those of us who aim to educate more students from the nation's most economically vulnerable communities, Berea provides a model that—though expensive—demonstrates what is possible with strong economic support to change lives for the better.

Centre College Acts Globally

Mark Twain once wrote: "Travel is fatal to prejudice, bigotry, and narrow-mindedness, and many of our people need it sorely on these accounts. Broad, wholesome, charitable views of men and things cannot be acquired by vegetating in one little corner of the earth all one's lifetime."[32] For many college students, arrival on campus can be their first long-term exposure to people who are markedly different than themselves. A key to growing up and preparing for entry into the responsibilities of citizenship is to reconcile the formative experiences of childhood with new impressions gained during college and through interactions with an ever-expanding world.

In parts of Kentucky, as in other areas of Appalachia or the south, students matriculating at college face pressures from those "left behind" who worry that students will forget where they came from or that they will prefer, once they've experienced a wider world, to never return home again. But Mark Twain's insight holds new meaning in the ever-connected global world that Thomas Friedman famously describes as "flat." Even as the world is at one's fingertips through technology, the ability to positively engage in a diverse world is continually expanding. Experience, however, intrudes upon preconceived ideas. Increased exposure to the world enhances empathy and diversifies perspectives, allowing one to build constructive unity out of diversity. Getting students out of their comfort zones, letting them—and even nudging them to—interact with others and find their way in the world, encourages growth that is not possible through other means.

Centre College, deeply committed to its broad-based liberal arts core, is equally dedicated to the notion that learning happens through stretching and, more specifically, dislocation. So, Centre makes it a priority to get students out into the world and, as appropriate, bring the world to the college's campus. In this way, Centre develops young adults' empathy and awareness as it sends students abroad and helps them graduate as global citizens.[33]

Global citizenship is promoted and, to the extent possible, measured by the Institute of International Education (IIE) and the US State Department's Bureau of Educational and Cultural Affairs in the annual Open Doors Report. The report documents internationalism on campus in multiple ways; it calculates the number of international students at US colleges and universities and also the number of US students who participate in international educational experiences, generally referred to as study abroad. The report for the 2015–2016 academic year shows that more than a million international students were studying in the United States, a 7 percent increase over previous years and the first time that milestone had been reached. Such a total also suggests that one of every twenty students on college campuses that year came to this country from abroad to study and learn.[34] More recent figures suggest that those numbers have dipped, but they still remain high relative to past decades.[35]

American students have been traveling overseas in greater numbers as well: 313,000 US students studied abroad during the 2014–2015 school year and received credit once they returned to their home institutions. About one-fourth of those students majored in STEM disciplines, and their travel supplemented the development of their technical expertise with a global awareness that cannot be attained in a classroom alone. As Evan Ryan, Assistant Secretary of State for Educational and Cultural Affairs, put it in the report, "International education helps people develop the knowledge and skills needed to succeed in today's global economy, and creates networks across borders that improve international understanding and strengthen the national security of the United States." Students, savvy about the ever-changing geopolitical scene, increasingly venture to such places as Cuba, Mexico, and Greece. Impressive as the totals may be, however, the numbers indicate that still only about 10 percent of all US undergrads study abroad even once by the time they graduate.[36] A great way to break down walls is to help students overcome personal barriers and create within countries an expanded population of global citizens. This opportunity is still not widely enough available.

Centre College directly takes on the challenge of increasing students' international awareness. Not content with seeing its bucolic setting in small-town Danville, Kentucky, as its borders, Centre strives to give every student who wishes to study overseas that opportunity. Relative to other institutions, the college is pretty good at meeting the goal: about 85 percent of the students at this college of about 1,400 study abroad at least once by the time they graduate.[37] Consequently, they regularly rank among the very best in the nation among colleges their size in numbers of undergraduates who study on foreign shores.[38] Students do not perceive study abroad as a mere requirement, they embrace it as a vital component of their education. In fact, more than 25 percent of the student body travel overseas more than once during their four years on campus.[39]

How does Centre College manage this internationalism-for-everyone expectation? The Centre Commitment is the college's promise that students will have at least one study abroad experience and an internship or research opportunity, and that they will graduate in four years or get their fifth year tuition free.[40] In support of the Commitment's first pillar, students are encouraged to think globally from the moment they arrive on campus. Any freshmen without a passport are provided one free of charge during their first year on campus.[41] The school's academic calendar favors access to travel as well. Many students enroll in a semester-long program during their junior year and travel overseas with Centre faculty to learn in a wide range of contexts. Students may also choose among numerous summer abroad programs, and they are eligible to spend multiple summers overseas. The short-semester January session, CentreTerm, is primarily dedicated to international education experiences both on campus and away. Students may travel overseas and are permitted to spend up to three different Januarys abroad.[42] And students who stay on campus during CentreTerm choose from among such courses as the following:

Global Migration;
Music and Culture of the African Diaspora;
Venetian Glass Techniques;
China's Modern Environmental History;
Borders and Cultural Encounters in Latin America;
Minority Cultures of Europe (the Laplanders, the Basques, and the Roma);
Consumer Culture, Globalization, and the Environment;
Japanese Culture in 16 Days

There are separate offerings in Latin American, Vietnamese, and French cinema, to name just a few.[43] Finally, some students augment their international experiences by merging the academic and the professional; students have arranged international internships across Africa, Brazil, China, Costa Rica, Honduras, Israel, Mexico, and Nicaragua.[44]

The focus, then, becomes all-encompassing. Students enroll at Centre College with the expectation that they will learn about themselves as they learn about the world, and that they will interact with the world in new ways. Centre feels an obligation to prepare students fully to face the world and, correspondingly, recognizes that helping develop global students will in turn positively impact the nation and their local communities. Centre's president, John A. Roush, maintains that "Centre takes seriously its mission to train global citizens, and not merely as a topic of academic study. Instead, the average 85 percent of our students who study abroad learn global citizenship first hand." Centre faculty design, plan, and teach overseas programs in a manner consistent with the liberal arts philosophy of the college, with small, interdisciplinary classes that bring together students from a variety of majors and minors.[45] The faculty cannot help but have their on-campus teaching influenced by their own international experiences; they become internationalized themselves. Students respond to the global perspective they encounter as freshmen and sophomores by immersing themselves in one or more new cultures by the time they graduate.[46]

Even those students (generally referred to, not disparagingly, as "the 15 percent") who somehow manage to reach graduation without ever studying abroad find their education deeply influenced by the college's global focus. The institution knows that the prevailing ethos—one of discovery, enlargement of perspective through encounters with different cultures, and diversity—is seamlessly integrated into campus life and the curriculum of each major. The college pursued grants several years ago and earned awards from the Mellon and the Arthur Vining Davis foundations to infuse the curriculum with global perspectives. New faculty positions; new global-oriented minors in Asian studies, Latin American studies, African and American studies, European studies, linguistics, and global commerce; and new courses throughout the curriculum translated Centre's international focus into a discernible transformation in Danville, Kentucky. The result is that Centre students, not just those who travel abroad, are "prepared for lives of learning, leadership, and service in a global community."[47]

University of Kentucky and the Commonwealth's Health

The early people of Kentucky were granted their wish of separating from the Commonwealth of Virginia when, on June 1, 1792, Kentucky became the fifteenth star on the flag of the United States of America. Despite its relatively modest geographic size (thirty-seventh in size by area), Kentucky is among the nation's top five in number of counties: 120 in total. This was done so that residents in far-flung areas could travel from their domiciles to their respective county seats and back within a day's journey. While the principle had enormous appeal in late eighteenth-century America, the duplication of services and facilities throughout Kentucky has become a contentious issue as obligations on the state and local governments have increased.

Meanwhile, in recent decades, Kentucky's health and wellness has suffered. Former University of Kentucky president Lee Todd referred to the Kentucky "uglies": the state's incidences of cancer, cardiovascular disease, stroke, obesity, diabetes, and unintentional injury. They are among the very worst in the country.[48] There are no simple fixes, even when the problems are painfully obvious and frustratingly public. But the state's flagship university has taken strategic steps and has responded repeatedly to conditions that threaten to cause public health crises.

Kentucky's problems, especially those in the relatively isolated, mountainous southeastern corner of the state, are part of the wellness concern that has spread through Appalachia and across much of the United States. Appalachia is considered "one of the nation's unhealthiest regions," based on "doctor shortages and access-to-care problems; stressful, unhealthy lifestyles; low education levels; and insidious poverty." Incredibly high rates of heart disease, diabetes, lung cancer, and obesity have come to define the region for public health experts. Those experts note that the region's residents combine poor health habits with "a sense of fatalism, that whatever happens, happens," which undermines innovative approaches to treatment and attempts to change the culture.[49]

This toxic mix, which education, cooperative, and cultural changes could hope to fix, threatens to blow what had once been seen as largely regional concerns into a broader crisis. The obesity–diabetes problem, for example, once considered a plight unique to the region and the lowest socioeconomic classes, is spreading.[50] Experts note, with increasing frustration, other enduring markers of poor health. Residents of Appalachia, especially those in its poorest counties, are far more likely to be diagnosed with diabetes, heart disease, and stroke than other Americans.[51] They exceed national levels on death rates related to coronary heart disease (by 15 to 21 percent), stroke (by 10 to 30 percent), and cancer (by up to 10 percent).[52]

Health workers in the area estimate that one-third of the population is diabetic and that, disturbingly, most do not even know it. These on-the-ground public health leaders now endorse radical approaches that involve community action and support for cultural change rather than tried-and-failed treatment approaches to individual health problems.[53] In other words, they are willing to consider anything to counter the identified barriers created by a health professional shortage in the region, less available commercial health insurance coverage, and an ingrained "fear, lack of knowledge, and distrust of the medical system."[54] The US Centers for Disease Control and Prevention (CDC) has identified a root cause of failed attempts to transform cultural tendencies that lends credibility to the gathering chorus of proposed interventions for patients who "gain most of their information about cancer from family, neighbors, and friends rather than from health professionals. Unfortunately, the information they receive often includes misperceptions of and dated knowledge about cancer treatments. The goal in Appalachia is to improve public career education while acknowledging and effectively using prevailing patterns of communication."[55]

The Commonwealth of Kentucky recognized the localized crisis conditions a generation ago and passed landmark legislation that empowered the University of Kentucky to deepen and diversify its health services to Appalachia and to other rural areas of the state. Grady Stumbo, the state's health secretary, and longtime state senator Benny Ray Bailey crafted Senate Bill 239 in 1990. The resulting law initiated funding for a University of Kentucky Center of Excellence in Rural Health, to be located in Hazard, Kentucky, in the heart of the mountains and deep in coal country, to address a critical physician shortage. In response, the university established residencies in Hazard in family and emergency medicine and critical care and started a program in health services research.

Later, a Master of Science in Nursing program, a Master of Social Work program, and undergraduate programs in Physical Therapy, Medical Technology, Clinical Leadership and Management, Clinical Laboratory Science, Medical Laboratory Science, and Social Work were added, as was an expansion of the Area Health Education Center (AHEC), all consistent with the codified mission of the Center of Excellence in Rural Health: "the improvement of the health of all rural Kentuckians and the improvement of rural health care systems through education, research, and service."[56] From its inception, the Center was designed to

Collect and maintain statistical and other information relating to rural health status, rural health care systems, rural health policy, and other issues affecting the health and well-being of rural populations;
Provide educational opportunities for students committed to rural health care: to obtain education in needed health professions as determined by the workforce analyses;
Maintain site-based family practice residencies; and
Demonstrate or provide innovative programs that improve the health of rural Kentuckians and strengthen rural health care systems.[57]

The University of Kentucky committed fully, investing in the Center of Excellence in Rural Health and, therefore, in the region's established medical facilities. They began training physicians and other health services professionals as well as the region's own people, including those from the area who were willing to remain in the area to provide medical care and those from the area who were in desperate need of the medical care that became available to them once Senate Bill 239 became law and the Center of Excellence in Rural Health became reality.

Over the past twenty-five years, then, the Center has had a deep impact on the health and well-being of eastern Kentucky by addressing identified concerns through physical or medicinal interventions and through facilitating shifts in cultural constructs. The center has been recognized as a national model for primary care and for rural health care. It has received regional and national grants for innovative practices and widespread recognition for dental outreach, diabetes interventions, and stroke studies. It has piloted research in diabetes, lung cancer, colorectal cancer, and patient advocacy. And the center has established partnerships with state and regional providers to enhance and expand services, introducing health career camps and forming community leadership institutes. In short, the Center of Excellence in Rural Health has transformed the way rural health care is done in the state and the nation. Along the way, the program has begun to reshape the internal and external perceptions of the region and has made a small but discernible dent in the health outcomes of a still-vulnerable population.

Pretty quickly, the Center of Excellence in Rural Health discovered that its biggest impact came through one of its simplest decisions: the formation of a tidy, dedicated operation called Kentucky Homeplace and the corresponding introduction of tireless, approachable grassroots advocates called Community Health Workers. The nationally recognized Homeplace program began in 1994 as a way for locals, mostly women, to provide nonclinical medical support and facilitation to encourage and, in many cases, translate the work of professional health service workers. Formally, the mission of Kentucky Homeplace is to "provide access to medical, social, and environmental services for the citizens of the Commonwealth," and its guiding vision is to "educate Kentuckians to identify risk factors and use preventative measures to become a healthier people with knowledge and skills to access the healthcare and social systems." Community Health Workers are trained to meet the medical needs of the region's residents in ways that meet them where they are. To improve access to appropriate services, they educate and inform patients about potentially confusing medical terminology, show them how to follow doctors' orders, and teach them to navigate the labyrinth of insurance and other financial barriers; when necessary, they remind patients of appointments or transport them to those appointments. They educate about preventive care and availability of services, general health and overcoming "social and cultural inhibitors," and self-management of disease.[58]

Community Health Workers are local and, according to the program, are employed from the communities in which they serve.[59] They are "family health care advisors."[60] In their advisory role they advocate for patients' "improved nutrition, increased physical activity, better weight management, smoking cessation, and improved diabetes self-management."[61] They go between health providers and patients to help identify risk factors and preventative measures. Because they are immersed in the patients' culture, they can effectively mediate unfamiliar or undesirable relationships with health professionals that may frustrate patients or even lead them not to pursue services. That familiarity and sense of comfort benefits individuals, and it increases the likelihood that clients will participate in health studies and remain engaged in those studies.[62]

The return on the investment in Community Health Workers is manifold. Community Health Workers find their own situations improved through their service. Their clients' lives are impacted. The health outlook, and, thus, all the corresponding factors of the region, start to change. So when the executive director of the Center of Excellence in Rural Health writes, "Policy change that advocates for Community Health Worker positions to be added to public health teams in underserved areas is needed," there is a good chance the state's legislators are listening.[63] It is certain that positive impacts such as the work of Community Health Workers and myriad other initiatives of the Center of Excellence in Rural Health do not go unnoticed.

The Commonwealth of Kentucky has a history of responding to the needs of its people. In many ways, that history of timely intervention is inseparable from the history of the state's flagship university since its foundation. Indeed, all of the state's institutions of higher education carry a demonstrable commitment to the people of the Commonwealth, meeting them where they are and rising together through education and service. Examples such as the University of Kentucky's Center of Excellence in Rural Health reveal the lengths to which these institutions go to address the pressing needs of individuals.

EKU Connects the State with the World

Partway through his excellent biography of Orville and Wilbur Wright and the story of their success in achieving flight in Kill Devil Hills, North Carolina, David McCullough describes the momentousness of their world-changing accomplishment:

> What had transpired that day in 1903, in the stiff winds and cold of the Outer Banks in less than two hours time, was one of the turning points in history, the beginning of change for the world far greater than any of those present could possibly have imagined. With their homemade machine, Wilbur and Orville Wright had shown without a doubt that man could fly and if the world did not yet know it, they did. Their flights that morning were the first ever in which a piloted machine took off under its own power into the air in full flight, sailed forward with no loss of speed, and landed at a point as high as that from which it started.[64]

Despite a deep belief in the fruits of their hard-earned success, there is no way the Wright brothers could have predicted that a little over a century later some 76,000 passenger flights would occur just in the United States every single day.[65] Airlines carried a record 849.3 million passengers in the United States in 2017, an average of more than 2 million fliers each day.[66] And another 12,000 estimated daily flights carry goods and freight or military personnel and equipment. The reality of the high-traffic skies led Bill Gates to call the airplane the first World Wide Web because of its ability to cross borders and bring people (as well as ideas, information, and materials) together.

Things show no signs of slowing down.

Aviation giant Boeing forecasts that over the next twenty years the airline industry will need more than a half-million new pilots to meet global demand.[67] Pilot training is intense; it requires hundreds, even thousands, of hours of supervised practice for licensure and there are rigorous standards for continued certification. Finding flight instructors is an expensive undertaking, and they are generally available only in highly populated areas with convenient access to up-to-date software and equipment, including, obviously, planes and runways. Eastern Kentucky University, with its aviation program's investment in sophisticated technology, unfettered access to a regional airport, and collaborative agreements that extend to communities and airports across the state, is doing its part to meet industry needs and the needs of the state's students.

EKU launched its aviation program in 1982, when it realized that the best aviation candidates were leaving the state to pursue an education.[68] After less than a decade, with the introduction of an aviation bachelor's degree and a Professional Flight option, the program took off. Other options in Aerospace Management and Aerospace Technology, and the addition of unmanned aerial vehicles (UAV) and helicopters, also provided opportunities for students who were broadly interested in the industry but were not aiming for a career as a pilot.[69] The 250–300 hours of flight time students accrue en route to their degree contributes to their attainment of Federal Aviation Administration (FAA) certification as private pilots and commercial pilots with ratings to fly single-engine and multiengine aircraft. Those experiences lead to jobs in the industry: graduates are pilots for commercial airlines, corporations, and the military; they become flight instructors and managers of airports and airlines; and they work as dispatchers or air traffic controllers.[70] The payoff has been rapid and widespread; the state is now "second in the nation in exporting aerospace goods and services."[71]

Today, the Eastern Kentucky University aviation program is defined by strategic and corporate partnerships with regional airlines and manufacturers and by educational partnerships with flight schools and with a growing number of the Commonwealth's community and technical colleges. Anticipated pilot shortages will threaten regional airlines first since major airlines hire from the ranks who get their start with regional companies. EKU Aviation has agreements with nine regional carriers, including PSA Airlines and Express Jets, and expects to add more such partnerships. The program's ambitious growth is reflected in uniquely tailored services for local students as well as for Korean and Chinese students, in anticipation of a heavy demand for pilots in Asia.[72] Partnerships include junior-year interviews with carriers such as Envoy Airlines, and some companies offer "pathway programs" that include the promise of postgraduation jobs, not just interviews.[73]

Those mutually beneficial relationships are not limited to air carriers. EKU announced late in 2016 that it had been chosen as one of five collegiate aviation programs to receive a new Cessna aircraft for training and recruitment purposes. The accompanying participation in the 2017 Top Hawk program strengthens EKU Aviation's support of students who desire summer internships with Textron Aviation, Cessna's parent company.[74] These opportunities diversify the University's offerings and match select students with "the world's leading aviation manufacturer" to expose them to innovative approaches in a rapidly evolving field and to give them opportunities to begin or advance careers.[75]

With a flexible and responsive program, Eastern Kentucky University's aviation major positions students to succeed. Graduates continue their education while they make progress toward the FAA-required 1,000 flight hours for advanced certification. Many EKU Aviation students begin their postsecondary education at a Kentucky Community and Technical College System campus. EKU, as mentioned, has partnered with community and technical colleges in Ashland in far eastern Kentucky, Hazard and Middlesboro in the southeastern corner of the state, and Owensboro in the Commonwealth's southwest region. These bridges serve the Commonwealth well, offering a way to extend associate's degrees in such programs as Airframes and Power Plants or Air Traffic Control with online courses that lead to the bachelor's degree; and the programs are supplemented with aviation courses taught by EKU-approved instructors in their local region.[76]

The goal is "to fly the EKU flag at every regional airport in the Commonwealth and across the United States." Communities promote the relationship because pilots are trained, degrees are earned, and students represent a brain gain.

Whether in aviation, rural health care, international education experiences, or providing low-income students with a high-income education, the colleges and universities in the Commonwealth have evolved to serve an important prosocial function within the state and community. They fill gaps in services often missed by the state or passed over by the market. These entities and their services act as essential institutional anchors in the broad mix of civil society institutions that help support a well-functioning republic.

Conclusion

Commonwealth at the Crossroads

Among his many works, noted Russian author Leo Tolstoy published an 1886 commentary about social conditions in his native Russia titled, *What Is to Be Done?* We pose the same question as we conclude. Recent trends do not portend a bright future in terms of state support for public campuses. The American Council on Education recently concluded that, given trends in state funding, the full "privatization" of public higher education in America, in which public levels of state support effectively reach zero, is on pace to happen by 2059, and possibly sooner.[1] Commentators have repeatedly warned that there is a growing higher education crisis among the most vulnerable pockets of the population due to waning state support.

Perhaps the most significant shift in the nation's economy over the past half-century has been the change from an economy driven primarily by agriculture, commodities, manufacturing, and natural resources to one in which services and technological innovation are increasingly outperforming these other areas. There is no better way to predict the nation's success in these emergent economic drivers than its educational achievement.

In a report focused on the Commonwealth of Massachusetts, and certainly applicable to any of our nation's state economies, researchers concluded:

> Higher education is the foundation for reliable economic growth in Massachusetts, and . . . increased funding for it makes sense. Although such a focus may at first glance appear to be out of concert with the current environment of recession and austerity, in fact public spending on higher education can provide both a short-run stimulus to ease the burden of unemployment and a long-run investment in an educated populace that will pay for itself in terms of higher wages, higher tax revenue, and lower public expenditures. The immediate benefits will reach many areas of the state's workforce, and the long-term benefits will continue to renew themselves. . . . In other words, a dramatic increase in the state's investment in public higher education is an exceptionally good deal for the entire Commonwealth and should be vigorously pursued by policy makers.[2]

In 2009, Nobel Prize–winning economist Paul Krugman wrote, "If you had to explain America's economic success with one word that word would be 'education.' . . . We need to wake up and realize that one of the keys to our nation's historic success is now a wasting asset. Education made America great; neglect of education can reverse the process."[3] In the preceding chapters, we have outlined the social and democratic underpinnings of public higher education and illustrated that the underpinnings of a successful representative government are linked to an educated populace. Consequently, we surveyed two of the pieces of legislation most important to the nation's progress—the Morrill Land-Grant Act and the GI Bill. The former helped establish public higher education institutions throughout America, while the latter threw open the doors to an entire generation who likely would have never enjoyed access to postsecondary education opportunities without legislative action.

The cumulative effect of these efforts is hard to overstate. Their common effect expanded the availability and affordability of education. That our citizens have gained their degrees at public colleges and universities, as opposed to private institutions, by an estimated ratio of 3 to 1 speaks to the consequence of these policies on the nation's progress. Today, however, it falls to the current generation, particularly lawmakers and those at public higher education institutions, which draw the large majority of American students, to ensure that those two essential elements of postsecondary education, access and affordability, continue to expand.[4] The public institutions these policies helped spawn are state and national treasures. They are also in dire need of support in order to continue to fulfill their role in society.

Postsecondary training, including a college degree, has become a prerequisite to expanded opportunity. Universities, through ever-more sophisticated scientific and technological discoveries, have contributed to an unprecedented age of prosperity in America.[5] The seeds planted by the Land-Grant Act and the GI Bill helped many first-generation college-going Americans earn degrees and improved the quality of life for subsequent generations of families and communities.

For Franklin Roosevelt, the United States of America owed those willing to sacrifice through military service a benefit that few men and women could then have hoped to access: a college education. To quote Roosevelt in the months leading up to the GI Bill's enactment, "the Nation is morally obligated to provide this training and education and the necessary financial assistance by which they can be secured."[6] Roosevelt's vision of access to education was of a piece with that of his predecessor Abraham Lincoln, who signed into law the Morrill Act of 1862. This Civil War–era legislation created numerous state colleges and universities throughout America, the vast majority of which were public schools. America can learn from these legislative triumphs.

Consider that during some of the most economically uncertain times of our nation's history—the Civil War and World War II—prescient lawmakers enacted two social policies that had the most impact on the democratization of postsecondary education. The legislators involved acted on a truth understood decades before by one of the most quotable of the Founders, Benjamin Franklin, who observed that the diffusion of public knowledge through libraries and books "improv'd the general Conversation of the Americans, made the common Tradesmen and Farmers as intelligent as most Gentlemen from other Countries, and perhaps have contributed in some degree to the Stand so generally made throughout the Colonies in Defense of their Privileges." In even more succinct terms, Franklin said on another occasion that "an investment in education always paid the best dividend."

William G. Bowen, president emeritus of the Andrew W. Mellon Foundation and Princeton University, and Michael S. McPherson, former president of the Spencer Foundation and Macalester College, put it this way: "There is probably no better-documented finding in the social sciences than that education pays. Studies across a wide variety of countries, with differing economic systems, examining different levels of education and employing a range of statistical techniques, have shown with mind-numbing consistency that the earnings differential between people with more education versus those with less education more than compensates students for the investment in time and money they make (or society makes on their behalf) in becoming more educated."[7] While it would be unreasonable to assume that these findings are all causal, it is also true that the connection between education and prosocial outcomes cannot be dismissed as merely a correlation.

To be sure, states today still invest in public higher education. It accounts for the third-largest expenditure of general fund budgets (the portion financed primarily through taxes) behind only primary and secondary education and Medicaid.[8] And, candidly, colleges and universities must do better to provide a better return on investment through strategic reforms. They must also improve communication about the good they do provide—who, after all, wants a surgeon without the proper training or an architect or engineer without a degree? While there is room to improve public higher education, there are, nonetheless, few better social investments.

Education is society's preventative medicine, as it equips individuals and families with the skills to succeed in an increasingly complex economic and social environment. As the nexus of the state's political, economic, social, and philosophical forces, public higher education is central to prepare society to shift in this direction. And yet many see higher education not as essential to shaping the future success of the state, but rather more as the "balance wheel" of state budgets, given that appropriations directed toward postsecondary institutions tend to rise disproportionately when the economy is strong and fall disproportionately when the economy is weak. Rather than having a vision, as with the Land-Grant Act and the GI Bill, for how higher education can reequip society to meet the challenges of a changing world, some lawmakers see higher education as an area that can be cut to help balance budgets and pay for other state services.

For better or worse, campuses are viewed as having both reserves (endowments) and revenue streams (tuition and philanthropic support) not readily available to other state agencies and are, therefore, viewed as better equipped to absorb cuts. Hence, privitization continues. Certainly, higher education institutions can change their program elements—even reduce degree offerings and increase class sizes, thus affecting the associated costs—in ways not possible for other state agencies.[9] But, notwithstanding the many demands on national and state budgets, elected officials should understand that support for American public education is of paramount importance to the republic's long-term success in terms of individual achievement and community growth.

Our country may face trade deficits in a whole host of areas, but higher education is not one of them. One need only examine the enrollment in graduate programs in the hard sciences to witness the world's demand for American higher education. Whether the rankings are determined by the *Times Higher Education* or *U.S. News and World Report,* the list of top global universities includes a preponderance of American institutions. To Jonathan Cole of Columbia University, the ambition to excel and the fierce competitiveness of scientists, scholars, and administrators at American research universities has led these entities to become the engines of our nation's prosperity. "The laser, magnetic resonance imaging, FM radio, the algorithm for Google searches, Global Positioning Systems, DNA fingerprinting, fetal monitoring, scientific cattle breeding, advanced methods of surveying public opinion, and even Viagra all had their origins in America's research universities, as did tens of thousands of other inventions, devices, medical miracles, and ideas that have transformed the world."[10] Clark Kerr, former president of the University of California, was correct in his assertion that the "United States has, overall, the most effective system of higher education the world has ever known."

A Brookings Institution study conducted for the *Wall Street Journal* found that, among sixteen geographic areas in which job growth was robust, despite a steep dip in manufacturing employment from 2000 to 2014, half housed major universities. Mark Muro, an urban specialist at Brookings, said: "Better educated places with colleges tend to be more productive and more able to shift out of declining industries into growing ones. Ultimately, cities survive by continually adapting their economies to new technologies, and colleges are central to that."[11]

Since the days of the Morrill Land-Grant Act and the GI Bill, America has made enormous investments in public higher education. In 2013, the government provided $157.5 billion in federal ($75.6 billion), state ($72.7 billion), and local ($9.2 billion) funds.[12] Federal investments, in the form of Pell Grants and Stafford loans direct to students, have been matched and in some cases exceeded by investments in infrastructure by state and local governments. One need only consider the *billions* invested in the form of classrooms, laboratories, residence halls, and the innumerable support structures needed to maintain a college or university to realize the imprudence of "walking back" our commitment to public institutions throughout our nation. These public investments in colleges and universities are augmented annually by private support. In 2016 contributions to higher education came from foundations ($12.45 billion), corporations ($6.6 billion), nonprofit organizations ($4.5 billion), alumni ($9.93 billion), and non-alumni individuals ($7.52 billion).[13] Add to this the $420 billion annually given to US higher education institutions in the form of tuition, fees, and room and board, and one gets a clearer picture of the enormity of the enterprise.[14]

All that said, this is not to suggest that closures or consolidations will never happen. Moody's Investor Service reported that closures of small colleges (which are defined by Moody's as private colleges with operating revenues below $100 million and public colleges below $200 million) are set to triple.

It appears the institutions most at risk are those in rural areas with small student populations that are leveraging their positions by increasing their discount rates. For many, this practice is not sustainable as discount rates—institutional grant dollars as a percentage of gross tuition and fee revenue—reached 48 percent for freshmen in 2014 at private colleges and universities. The fate of schools such as Sweet Briar in Virginia or St. Catharine in Kentucky might very well be more common as enrollment continues to dwindle at smaller, private institutions while the options at more affordable state universities prove attractive.

The National Center for Education Statistics reported that total undergraduate enrollment in degree-granting postsecondary institutions increased

31 percent, from 13.2 million in 2000 to 17.3 million in 2014. Even more significant for policy makers is that by 2025, total undergraduate enrollment is projected to increase to 19.8 million students.[15] And if these students are a reflection of the ever-changing American population, college campuses will grow increasingly diverse, thus ushering in an entire new wave of graduates— many of whom are first-generation—who have the potential to change the trajectory of their own lives and the prospects of those who will follow.

American public higher education, then, is at a crossroads. Once viewed as a public good and supported by a broad cross-section of local policy makers and communities, a college education is increasingly considered a "private benefit" by those who believe it should be treated as a consumption tax: those who use it, pay for it. Given the strains on state budgets across our country, we certainly understand this argument.

But when one considers that education represents some of the best medicine for the ills facing society and the best tool to address the opportunities ahead, wise communities will seek to increase investment and expand access rather than siphon resources in other directions. Demographics in the United States continue to change, and access to the American dream of postsecondary education—with the attendant promise of increased opportunities—should remain available to all those of ambition and able mind. America needs public policies for the twenty-first century that will have lasting impact on higher education in the tradition of the Land-Grant Act and the GI Bill of the nineteenth and twentieth centuries. Chapter 6 discusses systems like education that intervene early to treat root causes rather than symptoms.

In their recent work, *Lesson Plan: An Agenda for Change in American Higher Education,* scholars Bowen and McPherson call on faculty, administrators, and trustees—indeed, all those engaged in the educational enterprise—to be active in helping find solutions to address what will inevitably be the new normal for higher education in the coming decades. Collectively, the nation is up to the task. We take heart from a quotation from Alexis de Tocqueville in his *Democracy in America* (1835): "The greatness of America lies not in being more enlightened than any other nation, but rather in her ability to repair her faults."[16] Higher education can be repaired; and, in turn, higher education can help repair and lift individuals and communities. The words of the British prime minister Benjamin Disraeli apply as much to the United States and Kentucky today as they did to nineteenth-century Britain: "Upon the education of the people of this country, the fate of this country depends."[17]

Acknowledgments

The initial genesis of the book came after discussions between the authors at Yale Law School in November 2014. We first collaborated on an article that appeared in *Thought and Action,* the journal of the National Education Association. Further discussions and current events concerning higher education funding in Kentucky resulted in this expanded volume.

In recent years, we have watched some perceptions sour regarding institutions of higher education, as funds have also been trimmed. While some politicians and critics raise important concerns regarding the academy in Kentucky and elsewhere, such criticisms must be balanced by a better understanding of the vital role higher education continues to play in sustaining civil society.

This book speaks to policy makers, elected officials, and higher education's other constituencies; it makes the case that higher education is still worth public support and continued investment in Kentucky and beyond. In writing this book we have been encouraged and helped by many, and we wish to thank them for their respective roles in bringing this book to fruition.

We express our sincere appreciation to the president of West Virginia University, E. Gordon Gee, who generously agreed to provide the foreword and lend his name and reputation to our effort. During a long and distinguished career, Dr. Gee has led some of the great public and private institutions in America and is widely regarded as one of our nation's thought leaders when it comes to issues facing higher education. We are deeply honored to have him associated with our efforts. Several others reviewed the manuscript and provided helpful feedback throughout the process, including the late Gerald R. Sherratt, former president of Southern Utah University and mayor of Cedar City, Utah, and a giant in the landscape of western higher education. Dr. Sherratt passed away in July 2016 and is missed by all. We also thank Wayne Watkins for engaging with early writings that contributed to this manuscript.

The authors first heard a lecture titled "Lost Opportunities" by Professor James Klotter of Georgetown College and then were graciously provided a copy of the lecture, which helped coalesce our thoughts around events in Kentucky involving higher education. Interestingly enough, many of the events that have happened in Kentucky mirror larger trends within the United States. There are important lessons in what the Commonwealth has experienced. If we are to believe the statement above the entrance to the National Archives in Washington, DC, "The Past is Prologue," then what Professor Klotter outlines as lost opportunities from decades ago must be regarded as instructive lessons for those committed to eschewing the mistakes of the past concerning education.

Two Eastern Kentucky University colleagues and friends—Professor Gill Hunter and Jeremy Raines—proved invaluable with editing and formatting as we finalized our work, and we could not have completed this volume without their assistance. We are deeply indebted to both gentlemen for their efforts and encouragement. Professor Hunter's insights into Kentucky higher education, given his tenure at Eastern and his familiarity with the Commonwealth, proved extremely useful with chapter 7, in particular, as he made substantial contributions to the work. We thank research assistant Christian Sagers, who also provided important edits and suggestions throughout the manuscript. We thank Tom Appleton, a professor of history at Eastern, for his close reading and superb emendations.

We are deeply indebted to the University Press of Kentucky, specifically to its director Leila Salisbury and her incredible associates, Ila McEntire, Janet Yoe, Jackie Wilson, and Tasha Huber, for their belief in and support of this work and its timeliness. We certainly hope this book enhances the rich list of manuscripts and monographs that the Press produces each year and that our work helps add to the public discourse on higher education appropriations in Kentucky and other states around the nation.

We are thankful to the perceptive anonymous readers and reviewers who strengthened our analysis and thinking in several areas of the manuscript. Any errors or gaps in the text are our own and certainly not attributable to those who actively assisted in trying to craft a superior manuscript. Finally, and most importantly, we thank our respective spouses, Debi and Holly, and our families for their patience and forbearance as we worked on this book in addition to life's other day-to-day tasks. They were remarkably supportive. We do hope that our children and their peers might also someday be the beneficiaries of the world's greatest system of higher education.

Notes

Introduction

1. John Filson, "The Adventures of Col. Daniel Boone: The Discovery, Settlement, and Present State of Kentucke," in *Discovery, Settlement, and Present State of Kentucke* (1784) (New York: Cosimo, 2010).

2. Jill Barshay, "US Falls Behind Other Nations in the Global Knowledge Economy, Says 46-Country Report," *Higher Education*, November 24, 2015, accessed February 7, 2016, http://hechingerreport.org/us-falls-behind-other-nations-in-the-global-knowledge-economy-says-46-country-report/; see also Walter W. Powell and Kaisa Snellman, "The Knowledge Economy," *Annual Review of Sociology* 30:199–220 (August 2004). Noah Berger and Peter Fisher, "A Well-Educated Workforce is Key to State Prosperity," Economic Policy Institute, August 22, 2013, http://www.epi.org/publication/states-education-productivity-growth-foundations/.

3. Milken Institute, "State Tech and Science Index: State Ranking," accessed June 17, 2016, http://statetechandscience.org/state-ranking.html. Michael Mitchell and Michael Leachman, "Years of Cuts Threaten to Put College Out of Reach for More Students," Washington, DC: Center on Budget and Policy Priorities, May 13, 2013, accessed June 2, 2015, http://www.cbpp.org/research/years-of-cuts-threaten-to-put-college-out-of-reach-for-more-students.

4. Linda Blackford, "Bevin's Budget Spares K-12 Schools, Cuts Higher Education," *Lexington Herald-Leader,* January 26, 2016, http://www.kentucky.com/news/politics-government/article56718018.html.

5. Tom Loftus, "Pension Reform, Taxes and the Budget: Matt Bevin Reaches His Defining Moment as Governor," *Courier-Journal,* December 14, 2017, accessed December 20, 2017, https://www.courier-journal.com/story/news/2017/12/14/matt-bevin-kentucky-pension-reform-tax-reform-budget/897262001/.

6. Adam Beam, "Kentucky Governor Says State Budget 'Won't Be Pretty,'" Cincinnati, OH: WCPO-TV, December 21, 2017, accessed December 22, 2017, https://www.wcpo.com/news/state/state-kentucky/kentucky-governor-says-state-budget-wont-be-pretty.

7. "Gov. Bevin Proposes 9 Percent Cuts from Most State Agency Budgets," *Lane Report,* January 27, 2016, accessed June 17, 2016, http://www.lanereport.com/59419/2016/01/gov-bevin-proposes-9-percent-cuts-from-most-state-agency-budgets/.

8. "Gov. Bevin Proposes 9 Percent Cuts from Most State Agency Budgets." A report released from the Government Accountability Office also reveals that, from 2003 to 2012, state funding for public institutions of higher education "decreased by 12 percent overall while median tuition rose 55 percent across all public colleges." US Government Accountability Office, *Higher Education: State Funding Trends and Policies on Affordability,* GAO-15-151 (Washington, DC: GAO, 2014), ii, http://gao.gov/products/GAO-15-151.

9. Ellen Wexler, "State Support on the Rise," *Inside Higher Ed,* January 25, 2016, https://www.insidehighered.com/news/2016/01/25/state-support-higher-education-rises-41-percent-2016. Benjamin Snyder, "Student Loan Debt Has Increased—Again," *Fortune,* October 27, 2015, http://fortune.com/2015/10/27/student-loan-debt-increase/.

10. John Cheves, "Kentucky Teacher Pension Fund Liability Hits $24 Billion," *Lexington Herald-Leader,* December 9, 2015, accessed June 17, 2016, http://www.kentucky.com/news/politics-government/article48869495.html.

11. Brandon Busteed, "The Political Divide over Higher Education in America," Gallup Blog, *Gallup News,* December 12, 2017, accessed December 22, 2017, http://news.gallup.com/opinion/gallup/223451/political-divide-higher-education-america.aspx.

12. "Why Are Republicans Down on Higher Ed?," Education, *Gallup News,* accessed December 22, 2017, http://news.gallup.com/poll/216278/why-republicans-down-higher.aspx?g_source=link_newsv9&g_campaign=item_223451&g_medium=copy.

13. Hannah Fingerhut, "Republicans Skeptical of Colleges' Impact on U.S., but Most See Benefits for Workforce Preparation," Washington, DC: Pew Research Center, accessed December 22, 2017, http://www.pewresearch.org/fact-tank/2017/07/20/republicans-skeptical-of-colleges-impact-on-u-s-but-most-see-benefits-for-workforce-preparation/?utm_source=link_newsv9&utm_campaign=item_223451&utm_medium=copy.

14. Busteed, "The Political Divide over Higher Education in America."

15. Brody Mullins, Douglas Belkin, and Andrea Fuller, "Colleges Flex Lobbying Muscle," *Wall Street Journal,* November 8, 2015, http://www.wsj.com/articles/colleges-flex-lobbying-muscle-1447037474.

16. James C. Klotter, "What if . . .," *Kentucky Humanities,* no. 1 (2000).

17. James C. Klotter, "Lost Opportunities," speech in possession of authors, June 2015.

18. Klotter, "Lost Opportunities."

19. "From Thomas Jefferson to Joseph Carrington Cabell, 22 January 1820," *Founders Online,* National Archives, https://founders.archives.gov/documents/Jefferson/98-01-02-1031.

20. General Assembly, *Journal of the House of Representatives of the Commonwealth of Kentucky* (Frankfort, KY: Kendall and Russells, 1817), 295.

21. William E. Ellis, *A History of Education in Kentucky* (Lexington: University Press of Kentucky, 2011); James P. Cousins, *Horace Holley: Transylvania University and the Making of Liberal Education in the Early American Republic* (Lexington: University Press of Kentucky, 2016).

22. Susanna Delfino, Michele Gillespie, and Louis M. Kyriakoudes, *Southern Society and its Transformation, 1790–1860* (Columbia: University of Missouri Press, 2011), 179. See also Biographical Directory of the United States Congress, 1774–Present, http://bioguide.congress.gov/biosearch/biosearch.asp.

23. Klotter, "Lost Opportunities."

24. As one out-of-state higher education consultant commented on Twitter after the budget cuts were announced, "Kentucky has had a quietly strong #highered system. Bevin's proposed cuts will undermine that deeply." Susanna Williams, Twitter Post, January 26, 2016, https://twitter.com/susannadw/status/692149092420567040.

25. Daniel Walker Howe, *What Hath God Wrought: The Transformation of America, 1815–1848* (New York: Oxford University Press, 2007), 409.

26. Morrill Act of 1862, Pub. L. No. 37-108, 12 Stat. 503 (1862).

27. Michael T. Benson and Hal R. Boyd, "The *Public* University: Recalling Higher

Education's Democratic Purpose," *Thought & Action* (Summer 2015), http://www.nea.org/home/63441.htm.

28. Dwight D. Eisenhower, "Remarks at Annual Meeting of the Association of Land-Grant Colleges and Universities," November 16, 1954, *American Presidency Project,* online by Gerhard Peters and John T. Woolley, http://www.presidency.ucsb.edu/ws/?pid=10136.

29. Mary Anna Jackson, *Memoirs of Stonewall Jackson* (Louisville, KY: Prentice, 1895), 264.

30. Sandy Baum, Jennifer Ma, and Kathleen Payea, "Education Pays 2013: The Benefits of Higher Education for Individuals and Society," College Board, 2013, http://trends.collegeboard.org/sites/default/files/education-pays-2013-full-report-022714.pdf.

31. See, for example, Francis A. Young, "Educational Exchanges in the National Interest," *American Council of Learned Societies Newsletter* 20, no. 2 (March 1969): 1–18.

32. Richard Arum and Josipa Roksa, *Academically Adrift: Limited Learning on College Campuses* (Chicago: University of Chicago Press, 2011). Andrew Hacker and Claudia Dreifus, *Higher Education?: How Colleges Are Wasting Our Money and Failing Our Kids* (New York: St. Martin's Press, 2011). Clayton M. Christensen and Henry J. Eyring, *The Innovative University: Changing the DNA of Higher Education from the Inside Out* (San Francisco: Jossey-Bass, 2011). Richard H. Hersh and John Merrow, *Declining by Degrees: Higher Education at Risk* (New York: Palgrave Macmillan, 2005). Anthony T. Kronman, *Education's End: Why Our Colleges and Universities Have Given Up on the Meaning of Life* (Binghamton, NY: Vail-Ballou Press, 2007).

33. Josh Sanburn, "Higher Education Poll," *Time,* October 18, 2012, http://nation.time.com/2012/10/18/higher-education-poll/.

34. "Most Parents Expect Their Children to Attend College," Washington, DC: Pew Research Center, February 27, 2012, accessed March 23, 2015, http://www.pewresearch.org/daily-number/most-parents-expect-their-children-to-attend-college/.

35. Paul Fain, "The New Bachelor's Payoff," *Inside Higher Ed,* February 11, 2015, accessed June 2, 2015, https://www.insidehighered.com/news/2015/02/11/bachelors-degrees-lead-employment-and-more-training.

36. Matthew T. Lambert, *Privatization and the Public Good* (Cambridge, MA: Harvard University Education Press, 2014).

37. E. C. Lagemann and H. Lewis, *What Is College For? The Public Purpose of Higher Education* (New York: Teachers College Press, 2011). John Saltmarsh and Matthew Hartley, *"To Serve a Larger Purpose": Engagement for Democracy and the Transformation of Higher Education* (Philadelphia: Temple University Press, 2011).

38. Michael S. Roth, *Beyond the University: Why Liberal Education Matters* (New Haven, CT: Yale University Press, 2014). Martha C. Nussbaum, *Not for Profit: Why Democracy Needs the Humanities* (Princeton, NJ: Princeton University Press, 2010).

39. Charles Dorn, *For the Common Good: A New History of Higher Education in America* (Ithaca, NY: Cornell University Press, 2017), 236.

40. See, generally, work by Charles Sabel, including Sabel and William Simon, "Minimalism and Experimentalism in the Administrative State," *Georgetown Law Journal* 100, no. 1 (2011); Sabel, AnnaLee Saxenian, Reijo Miettinen, Peer Hull Kristensen, and Jarkko Hautamäki, *Individualized Service Provision as the Key to the New Welfare State: Lessons from Special Education in Finland* (Helsinki: Sitra, 2011); Sabel, "Dewey, Democracy and Democratic Experimentalism," *Contemporary Pragmatism* 9, no. 2 (2012); Sabel, Grainne de Burca, and Robert O. Keohane, "Global Experimentalist Governance," *British Journal*

of Political Science 44, no. 3 (2014); Sabel and Jonathan Zeitlin, "Experimentalism in the EU: Common Ground and Persistent Differences," *Regulation & Governance* 6 (2012): 410–426; Sabel and Jonathan Zeitlin, "Experimentalist Governance," in *The Oxford Handbook of Governance,* ed. David Levi-Faur (New York: Oxford University Press, 2012), 169–186; Sabel, "Individualised Service Provision and the New Welfare State: Are There Lessons from Northern Europe for Developing Countries?," in *Promoting Inclusive Growth: Challenges and Policies,* ed. Luiz de Mello and Mark A. Dutz (Paris: OECD Publishing, 2012).

41. Mullins, Belkin, and Fuller, "Colleges Flex Lobbying Muscle."

42. Daniel Mallory, ed., *The Life and Speeches of the Hon. Henry Clay* (New York: Yale R.P. Bixby & Company, 1843), 250.

1. The Democratic Ethos of Higher Education

1. The former quotation is attributed to Robert Maynard Hutchins, former president of the University of Chicago, and the latter comes from Clark Kerr, former president of UC Berkeley. See Clark Kerr, *The Uses of the University* (Cambridge, MA: Harvard University Press, 2001), 15.

2. A majority of states now allocate at least some funding for higher education based on institutional performance matrix. See National Conference of State Legislators, "Performance-Based Funding for Higher Education," last modified July 31, 2015, Washington, DC: NCSL, accessed June 22, 2016, www.ncsl.org/research/education/performance-funding.aspx.

3. Martha Stassen, Anne Herrington, and Laura Henderson, "Defining Critical Thinking in Higher Education," in *To Improve the Academy: Resources for Faculty, Instructional, and Organizational Development,* ed. Judith E. Miller and James Groccia (San Francisco, CA: Jossey-Bass, 2011), 30:126.

4. See, generally, Daniel F. Chambliss, *How College Works* (Cambridge, MA: Harvard University Press, 2014).

5. Derek Bok, *Higher Education in America* (Princeton, NJ: Princeton University Press, 2013).

6. Benjamin Franklin, *Proposals Relating to the Education of Youth in Pensilvania* (Philadelphia: 1749); Penn University Archives and Records Center, http://www.archives. upenn.edu/primdocs/1749proposals.html.

7. Bok, *Higher Education in America,* 29.

8. This second Land-Grant Act presents an interesting conflict in the democratizing of education in the United States, in part, because of its compromise on social justice. The practical effect of the law was that some states opted to establish HBCUs rather than integrate their students. Such schools were, by nature, separate but unequal institutions of learning. This history is complex and merits a more comprehensive treatment than we provide in the scope of this work. We recommend Bobby L. Lovett's recent work *America's Historically Black Colleges and Universities: A Narrative History, 1837–2009* (Macon, GA: Mercer University Press, 2015).

9. Daniel Coit Gilman, "Inaugural Address of Daniel Coit Gilman as First President of The Johns Hopkins University," The Johns Hopkins University, Baltimore, MD, February 22, 1876.

10. Philo Hutcheson, "The Truman Commission's Vision of the Future," *Thought & Action: The NEA Higher Education Journal* (Fall 2007): 107–115.

11. Thomas Jefferson founded one of the first public universities in the United States,

the University of Virginia. He considered the university, including its iconic architectural design, one of his greatest accomplishments in life. There he also developed a unique model for higher education that equipped leaders with tools for political participation and allowed students to elect courses. Jefferson's passion for a civic-minded education is best captured in his famous "Bill for the More General Diffusion of Knowledge." While the Virginia legislative proposal did not pass, it still serves to document Jefferson's vision for education in the Republic. "It is believed," he said, "that the most effectual means of preventing [Tyranny] would be to illuminate, as far as practicable, the minds of the people at large. . . . It is generally true that people will be happiest whose laws are best, and are best administered, and that laws will be wisely formed, and honestly administered, in proportion as those who form and administer them are wise and honest; whence it becomes expedient for promoting the public happiness that those persons, whom nature hath endowed with genius and virtue, should be rendered by liberal education worthy to receive, and able to guard the sacred deposit of the rights and liberties of their fellow citizens." See "A Bill for the More General Diffusion of Knowledge, 18 June 1779," *Founders Online*, National Archives, http://founders.archives.gov/documents/Jefferson/01-02-02-0132-0004-0079, last updated March 28, 2016. Source: *The Papers of Thomas Jefferson*, vol. 2, *1777–18 June 1779*, ed. Julian P. Boyd (Princeton, NJ: Princeton University Press, 1950), 526–535. For more on Jefferson's views on education and the early Republic, see, generally, Michael Roth, *Beyond the University: Why Liberal Education Matters* (New Haven, CT: Yale University Press, 2014).

12. See "George Washington to the Commissioners of the Federal District, January 28, 1795," *The Writings of George Washington: 1794–1798*, vol. 13, ed. Worthington Chauncey Ford (New York: G. P. Putnam's Sons, 1892), 36. See also "George Washington to Thomas Jefferson, March 15, 1795," *The Writings of George Washington: 1794–1798*, 13:51.

13. Joseph Ellis, *His Excellency: George Washington* (New York: Alfred A. Knopf, 2004), 9.

14. George Thomas, *The Founders and the Idea of a National University: Constituting the American Mind* (Cambridge: Cambridge University Press, 2014) and Albert Castel, "The Founding Fathers and the Vision of a National University," *History of Education Quarterly* 4, no. 4 (1964): 280–302.

15. George Washington, "First Annual Message to Congress on the State of the Union," January 8, 1790, *American Presidency Project*, online by Gerhard Peters and John T. Woolley, www.presidency.ucsb.edu/ws/?pid=29431.

16. George Washington, "To John Adams from George Washington, 15 November 1794," *Founders Online*, National Archives, http://founders.archives.gov/documents/Adams/99-02-02-1585.

17. George Washington, "Eighth Annual Message," December 7, 1796, *American Presidency Project*, online by Gerhard Peters and John T. Woolley, www.presidency.ucsb.edu/ws/?pid=29438.

18. George Washington, "To Alexander Hamilton, September 1, 1796," *The Writings of George Washington: 1794–1798*, 13: 267; and Alexander Hamilton, "From Alexander Hamilton to George Washington, September 4, 1796," *The Papers of Alexander Hamilton: January 1796-March 1797*, vol. 20, ed. Harold C. Syrett (New York: Columbia University Press, 1974), 316.

19. George Washington, "George Washington's Last Will and Testament, July 9, 1799," *The Papers of George Washington, Retirement Series*, vol. 4, ed. W. W. Abbot (Charlottesville: University Press of Virginia), 479–511.

20. The Northwest Ordinances of 1785 and 1787, two of the few legislative success-

es of the Confederation Congress, paved the way for new states to enter the Union. The 1785 ordinance specified that a section of each new township should be rented to a settler whose payments were to fund and maintain public schools. The desire for public schooling was further emphasized in the 1787 ordinance, which declares that in the new territory, "Religion, morality, and knowledge, being necessary to good government and the happiness of mankind, schools and the means of education shall forever be encouraged." These laws could help explain how townships and states, rather than the national government, assumed the task of providing public education early in the country's history.

21. Carl F. Kaestle, "Public Education in the Old Northwest: 'Necessary to Good Government and the Happiness of Mankind,'" *Indiana Magazine of History* 84, no. 1 (March 1988): 60–74.

22. Art. 3 in "Transcript of Northwest Ordinance (1787)," Our Documents, accessed December 6, 2017, https://www.ourdocuments.gov/doc.php?flash=false&doc=8&page=transcript.

23. Of note is that the Ordinances of 1785 and 1787, and their directives on public education, included only the territory northwest of the Ohio River and thus excluded what would become the Commonwealth of Kentucky.

24. Kevin Carey, "Fulfill George Washington's Last Wish—A National University," Atlanta, GA: CNN, March 2, 2015, accessed June 1, 2015, www.cnn.com/2015/03/02/opinion/carey-george-washington-wish-national-university.

25. Morrill Act of 1862, Pub. L. 37-108, 12 Stat. 503 (1862).

26. Coy Cross, *Justin Smith Morrill: Father of Land-Grant Colleges* (Lansing: Michigan State University Press, 1999), 5.

27. Morrill to James Barrett, January 1886, Library of Congress, as cited in Cross, *Justin Smith Morrill*, 6.

28. Justin Morrill, "Speech of Hon. Justin S. Morrill, of Vermont, on the Bill Granting Lands for Agricultural Colleges; Delivered in the House of Representatives, April 20, 1858" (speech, Washington, DC: Congressional Globe Office, 1858).

29. US Congress, Senator Harlan of Iowa. 35th Cong., 2d sess. Congressional Globe (February 1, 1859): 720; http://www.memory.loc.gov:8081/cgi-bin/ampage?collId=llcg&fileName=049/llcg049.db&recNum=763.

30. Edward Danforth Eddy, *Colleges for Our Land and Time: The Land-Grant Idea in American Education* (New York: Harper, 1957), 45, as cited in Cross, *Justin Smith Morrill*, 88.

31. Dwight Eisenhower, "Remarks at Annual Meeting of the Association of Land-Grant Colleges and Universities," November 16, 1954. *American Presidency Project*, online by Gerhard Peters and John T. Woolley, accessed June 1, 2015, www.presidency.ucsb.edu/ws/?pid=10136.

32. Suzanne Mettler, *Soldiers to Citizens: The GI Bill and the Making of the Greatest Generation* (London: Oxford University Press, 2005), 42.

33. US Department of Veterans Affairs, "Born of Controversy: The GI Bill of Rights," accessed June 24, 2016, https://www.va.gov/opa/publications/celebrate/gi-bill.pdf.

34. Mettler, *Soldiers to Citizens*, 42.

35. "Letter, Harry S. Truman to Bess Wallace, June 27, 1918," *Family, Business, and Personal Affairs File, Truman Papers*, Harry S. Truman Presidential Library and Museum, accessed June 24, 2016, www.trumanlibrary.org/whistlestop/study_collections/ww1/documents/index.php?documentdate=1918-06-27&documentid=1-10&studycollectionid=&pagenumber=1.

36. Harry Truman, "Commencement Address at Howard University," June 13, 1952, *American Presidency Project*, online by Gerhard Peters and John T. Woolley, accessed June 24, 2016, www.presidency.ucsb.edu/ws/?pid=14160.

37. Sarah Gibson Blanding, "The Dean's Contribution to the Life of Our Times," *Journal of the National Association of Deans of Women* 9, no. 4 (Summer 1946): 148.

38. Sarah Gibson Blanding, "Edward R. Murrow Interviews Sarah Blanding, 1959," YouTube video, accessed July 5, 2016, https://www.youtube.com/watch?v=pHNopOwrHxc (see 11:38).

39. Adelaide Kerr, "Vassar's President is Full of New Educational Ideas," *Milwaukee Journal*, April 23, 1946, 16; https://news.google.com/newspapers?nid=1499&dat=19460423&id=xkYaAAAAIBAJ&sjid=LCUEAAAAIBAJ&pg=4674,3039397&hl=en.

40. Harry Truman, "Letter Appointing Members to the National Commission on Higher Education," July 13, 1946, *American Presidency Project*, online by Gerhard Peters and John T. Woolley, accessed June 24, 2016, www.presidency.ucsb.edu/ws/?pid=12452.

41. Julie A. Reuben and Linda Perkins, "Introduction: Commemorating the Sixtieth Anniversary of the President's Commission Report, Higher Education for Democracy," *History of Education Quarterly* 47, no. 3 (August 2007): 265–276.

42. The President's Commission on Higher Education, *Establishing the Goals.* Vol. 1 of *Higher Education for American Democracy: A Report of the President's Commission on Higher Education* (Washington, DC: US Government Printing Office, 1947), 25.

43. William Du Bois, "The Freedom to Learn," in *W. E. B. Du Bois Speaks: Speeches and Addresses, 1920–1963*, ed. Philip. S. Foner (New York: Pathfinder Press, 1970), 230–231.

44. Commission on Higher Education, *Establishing the Goals,* 29.

45. Harry Truman, "Statement by the President Making Public a Report of the Commission on Higher Education," December 15, 1947, *American Presidency Project*, online by Gerhard Peters and John T. Woolley, accessed June 24, 2016, www.presidency.ucsb.edu/ws/?pid=12802.

46. Kerr, "Vassar's President is Full of New Educational Ideas."

47. The President's Commission on Higher Education, "Equalizing and Expanding Individual Opportunity." Vol. 2 of *Higher Education for American Democracy: A Report of the President's Commission on Higher Education* (Washington, DC: US Government Printing Office, 1942), 3.

48. "College ROI Report: Best Value Colleges," *Pay Scale, Inc.*, accessed June 1, 2015, www.payscale.com/college-roi/.

49. See Sandy Baum, Jennifer Ma, and Kathleen Payea, "Education Pays 2013: The Benefits of Higher Education for Individuals and Society," College Board, 2013, accessed June 24, 2016, http://trends.collegeboard.org/sites/default/files/education-pays-2013-full-report-022714.pdf.

50. Baum, Ma, and Payea, "Education Pays 2013."

51. The Guardians Initiative, *Return on Investment in College Education*, Association of Governing Boards of Universities and Colleges, https://www.agb.org/reports/2017/return-on-investment-in-college-education.

52. US research universities account for 11 of the top 20 global institutions ranked for scientific research by the journal *Nature*. See "Nature Index Tables: Table 2: Top 200 Institutions," *Nature* 522 (June 2015): S34–S44, accessed June 1, 2015, https://www.nature.com/articles/522S34a/tables/2.

53. Margaret Cahalan and Laura Perna, "Indicators of Higher Education Equity in

the United States," Pell Institute for the Study of Opportunity in Higher Education and The University of Pennsylvania Alliance for Education and Democracy, 2015, https://files.eric. ed.gov/fulltext/ED555865.pdf, 30.

54. In scrutinizing the methodology of the Pell Institute's study, cited above, Matthew Chingos of the Brookings Institution and Susan Dynarski of the University of Michigan estimate that the college graduation rate for the top income quartile is closer to 54 percent while the lowest quintile is closer to 17 percent. See Matthew M. Chingos and Susan M. Dynarski, "How Can We Track Trends in Educational Attainment by Parental Income? Hint: Not with the Current Population Survey," Brookings Institution, 2015, accessed June 24, 2016, http://www.brookings.edu/research/papers/2015/03/12-chalkboard-income-education-attainment-chingos and http://www.brookings.edu/research/papers/2015/03/12-chalk boardincome-education-attainment-chingos#_end1. In their 2011 working paper, Bailey and Dynarski demonstrate "that inequality in college persistence explains a substantial share of inequality in college completion. These differences in persistence may be driven by financial, academic, and social factors." See Martha J. Bailey and Susan M. Dynarski, "Gains and Gaps: Changing Inequality in U.S. College Entry and Completion," National Bureau of Economic Research, 2011, accessed June 24, 2016, http://users.nber.org/~dynarski/Bailey _Dynarski.pdf.

55. William English Kirwan, "Keynote Address Delivered at University of Kentucky Sesquicentennial, February 23, 2015," University of Kentucky, accessed June 24, 2016, http://uknow.uky.edu/content/u-k-0.

56. Kellie Woodhouse, "A Career's Worth of Change," *Inside Higher Ed,* July 14, 2015, accessed December 22, 2017, https://www.insidehighered.com/news/2015/07/14/exit-in terview-outgoing-university-system-maryland-chancellor-brit-kirwan.

2. "Univercities" and the Soul of the Student-Citizen

1. Many of the original twelve corporations in the Dow Jones Industrial Average still exist in some form. Most, however, have gone through name changes and buyouts and have changed industries. Of the original twelve, one corporation remains on the Dow Jones Industrial Average today: General Electric.

2. John Dewey, *Democracy and Education* (Brooklyn, NY: Sheba Blake, 2015), 3.

3. See Michael Roth, *Beyond the University: Why Liberal Education Matters* (New Haven, CT: Yale University Press, 2014).

4. See *The Report of the President's Commission on Campus Unrest,* William Scranton, chair, 1970, https://files.eric.ed.gov/fulltext/ED083899.pdf.

5. See, generally, Anthony T. Kronman, *Education's End: Why Our Colleges and Universities Have Given Up on the Meaning of Life* (New Haven, CT: Yale University Press, 2007).

6. Frank Klassen, "Persistence and Change in Eighteenth Century Colonial Education," *History of Education Quarterly* 2, no. 83 (June 1962): 83. See also Franklin Rudolph, *The American College and University* (Athens, GA: University of Georgia Press, 2011), 62–63.

7. Rudolph, *The American College and University,* 84.

8. John Thelin, Jason R. Edwards, Eric Moyen, Joseph B. Berger, and Maria V. Calkins, "Higher Education in the United States—Historical Development, System," *Education Encyclopedia,* accessed July 8, 2016, http://education.stateuniversity.com/pages/2044/High er-Education-in-United-States.html.

9. Jonathan R. Cole, *The Great American University: Its Rise to Preeminence, Its Indispensable Role, Why It Must Be Protected* (New York: Public Affairs, 2009), 18.

10. Cole, *The Great American University*, 20–21.

11. Abraham Flexner, *Daniel Coit Gilman: Creator of the American Type of University* (New York: Harcourt, Brace, 1946), 105–106.

12. Flexner, *Daniel Coit Gilman*.

13. Flexner, *Daniel Coit Gilman*.

14. Clark Kerr, *The Uses of the University* (Cambridge, MA: Harvard University Press, 2001), 31.

15. Aristotle, *Politics* 1337a10.

16. Aristotle, *Ethics* 1103b25.

17. Citizens, in Aristotle's view and in Athens, were exclusively adult males. Aristotle did not believe that women, children, or slaves were fit for political participation. Although we endorse many of Aristotle's views, suffice it to say that time has most certainly proven him wrong on this and other accounts.

18. Ian Morris, *Burial and Ancient Society* (New York: Cambridge University Press, 1987), 100.

19. Morris, *Burial and Ancient Society*, 31.

20. Christopher P. Loss, *Between Citizens and the State: The Politics of American Higher Education in the 20th Century* (Princeton, NJ: Princeton University Press, 2014), 214.

21. See "The Rising Cost of Not Going to College," Pew Research Center, February 11, 2014, http://www.pewsocialtrends.org/2014/02/11/the-rising-cost-of-not-going-to-college/. See also "The Economics of Higher Education," A Report Prepared by the Department of the Treasury with the Department of Education, December 2012, https://www.treasury.gov/connect/blog/Documents/20121212_Economics%20of%20Higher%20Ed_vFINAL.pdf.

22. Abraham Flexner, *Universities: American, English, German* (New York: Oxford University Press, 1930), 196.

23. "The college is . . . not to be regarded as a training school" from Abraham Flexner, *The American College; A Criticism* (New York: The Century Co., 1908), 136. See Ronald F. Movrich, "Before the Gates of Excellence: Abraham Flexner and Education, 1866–1918" (PhD diss., University of California, Berkeley, 1981).

24. Robert Maynard Hutchins, *The Higher Learning in America* (New Brunswick, NJ: Transaction, 1995), 69–70.

25. Roth, *Beyond the University*.

26. "A Bill for the More General Diffusion of Knowledge, 18 June 1779," *Founders Online*, National Archives, last modified June 29, 2016, http://founders.archives.gov/documents/Jefferson/01-02-02-0132-0004-0079. [Original source: *The Papers of Thomas Jefferson*, vol. 2, *1777–18 June 1779*, ed. Julian P. Boyd (Princeton, NJ: Princeton University Press, 1950), no pagination.]

27. "A Bill for the More General Diffusion of Knowledge, 18 June 1779."

28. Benjamin Franklin, *The Writings of Benjamin Franklin*, vol. 2, ed. Henry Albert Smyth (New York: Macmillan, 1905), 391.

29. David Brooks, "The Big University," *New York Times*, October 6, 2015, http://www.nytimes.com/2015/10/06/opinion/david-brooks-the-big-university.html?_r=0.

30. Brooks, "The Big University."

31. David F. Chambliss and Christopher G. Takacs, *How College Works* (Cambridge, MA: Harvard University Press, 2014), 16.

32. Abigail Hess, "Harvard Business School Professor: Half of American Colleges Will Be Bankrupt in 10 to 15 Years," *CNBC MakeIt,* November 15, 2017, https://www.cnbc.com/2017/11/15/hbs-professor-half-of-us-colleges-will-be-bankrupt-in-10-to-15-years.html.

33. Tamar Lewin, "What Makes a Positive College Experience," *New York Times,* April 11, 2014, http://www.nytimes.com/2014/04/13/education/edlife/what-makes-a-positive-college-experience.html?_r=0.

34. Vincent Tinto, *Leaving College: Rethinking the Causes and Cures of Student Attrition* (Chicago: University of Chicago Press, 1993).

35. See Emile Durkheim, *Le Suicide* (Paris: F. Alcan, 1897).

36. Jeremy Ashkenas, Haeyoun Park, and Adam Pearce, "Even with Affirmative Action, Blacks and Hispanics Are More Underrepresented at Top Colleges Than 35 Years Ago," *New York Times,* August 24, 2017, https://www.nytimes.com/interactive/2017/08/24/us/affirmative-action.html.

37. Thomas F. Pettigrew and Linda R. Tropp, "A Meta-Analytic Test of Intergroup Contact Theory," *Journal of Personality and Social Psychology* 90, no. 5 (May 2006): 751–783.

38. Aristotle, *Ethics* 1103(a)(30).

39. Aristotle, *Politics* 1253a30.

3. Higher Education and the Fourth Estate

1. James Baldwin, "Autobiographical Notes," in *James Baldwin: Collected Essays,* ed. T. Morrison (New York: Library of America, 1998), accessed July 13, 2016, https://www.nytimes.com/books/first/b/baldwin-essays.html.

2. Eli Kintisch, "Writer Wendell Berry Takes Aim at the Modern Research University," *Science Magazine,* June 24, 2010, accessed July 14, 2016, http://www.sciencemag.org/news/2010/06/writer-wendell-berry-takes-aim-modern-research-university.

3. "Wendell E. Berry Interview," National Endowment for the Humanities, 2012, accessed July 14, 2016, http://www.neh.gov/about/awards/jefferson-lecture/wendell-e-berry-interview.

4. David Skinner, "Wendell E. Berry Biography," National Endowment for the Humanities, May/June 2012, accessed July 14, 2016, http://www.neh.gov/about/awards/jefferson-lecture/wendell-e-berry-biography.

5. Melissa Walker, "'Havens for Golf-Turf Science': New Agrarians and the Land-Grant Legacy," in *Service as Mandate: How American Land-Grant Universities Shaped the Modern World, 1920–2015,* ed. Alan I. Marcus (Tuscaloosa, AL: University of Alabama Press, 2015), 280.

6. Matt Bonzo and Michael Stevens, "Seed Will Sprout in the Scar: Wendell Berry on Higher Education," *Other Journal,* August 13, 2008, http://theotherjournal.com/2008/08/13/seed-will-sprout-in-the-scar-wendell-berry-on-higher-education/.

7. Wendell Berry, "Higher Education and Home Defense," in *Home Economics: Fourteen Essays of Wendell Berry* (Berkeley, CA: Counterpoint, 1987).

8. Harold T. Shapiro, "The University and Society," in *A Larger Sense of Purpose: Higher Education and Society* (Princeton, NJ: Princeton University Press, 2005), 4.

9. Thomas Carlyle, "Lecture V: The Hero as Man of Letters. Johnson, Rousseau,

Burns," in *On Heroes, Hero-Worship, & the Heroic in History. Six Lectures. Reported with emendations and additions* (London: J. M. Dent & Sons, 1908), 392.

10. Carlyle, "Lecture V: The Hero as Man of Letters."

11. Robert H. Bork, "Address at the Philanthropy Roundtable's First Annual Meeting," Philanthropy Roundtable, October 1992, accessed July 11, 2016, http://www.philanthropy-roundtable.org/topic/donor_intent/interpreting_the_founders_vision.

12. Michelle Stack, "Journalists and Academics as Public Educators," *Academic Matters*, May 2011, accessed July 12, 2016, http://www.academicmatters.ca/2011/05/journalists-and-academics-as-public-educators/.

13. "From Thomas Jefferson to Adamantios Coray, 31 October 1823," *Founders Online*, National Archives, last modified June 29, 2016, http://founders.archives.gov/documents/Jefferson/98-01-02-3837.

14. Thomas Jefferson, "Preamble to a Bill for the More General Diffusion of Knowledge," chap. 18, document 11 in *The Founder's Constitution*, Fall 1778 (web edition, University of Chicago Press and the Liberty Fund), accessed July 11, 2016, http://press-pubs.uchicago.edu/founders/documents/v1ch18s11.html.

15. Mark Hoekstra, Steven L. Puller, and Jeremy West, "Cash for Corollas: When Stimulus Reduces Spending," National Bureau of Economic Research, Working Paper no. 20349, July 2014.

16. Michael Sivak and Brandon Schoettle, "The Effect of the 'Cash for Clunkers' Program on the Overall Fuel Economy of Purchased New Vehicles," Technical report UM-TRI-2009-34. (Ann Arbor: Transportation Research Institute at the University of Michigan, 2009).

17. John E. Sununu, "Cash for Clunkers: How Bad Public Policy Gets Made," *Boston Globe*, September 1, 2014.

18. David Leonhardt, "Be Warned: Mr. Bubble's Worried Again," *New York Times*, August 21, 2005, http://www.nytimes.com/2005/08/21/business/yourmoney/be-warned-mr-bubbles-worried-again.html. See also Karl E. Case and Robert J. Shiller, "Is There a Bubble in the Housing Market?," *Brookings Papers on Economic Activity* 34, no. 2 (2003): 299.

19. Bofta Yinam, "Delay Claims on PennDOT Projects Cost Taxpayers Millions," *Pittsburgh Action 4 News*, Pittsburgh: WTAE-TV, July 23, 2015, http://www.wtae.com/news/delay-claims-on-penndot-projects-cost-taxpayers-millions/34321364.

20. Dug Begley, "Lawmakers Demand Fix for Utility-Related Road Delays," *Houston Chronicle*, August 12, 2015, http://www.houstonchronicle.com/news/transportation/article/Lawmakers-demand-fix-for-utility-related-road-6441050.php. Mike Frassinelli, "DOT: Delays Moving Utilities Costing N.J. Tens of Millions Per Year," *Star-Ledger*, March 16, 2013, http://www.nj.com/news/index.ssf/2013/03/dot_delays_in_moving_utilities.html. "Transportation Infrastructure: Impacts of Utility Relocations on Highway and Bridge Projects" (Washington, DC: General Accounting Office, June 1999), http://www.gao.gov/archive/1999/rc99131.pdf.

21. Roy E. Sturgill, Timothy R. B. Taylor, Seyedmahdi Ghorashinezhad, and Jiwen Zhang, "Methods to Expedite and Streamline Utility Relocations for Road Projects," Lexington: University of Kentucky, Kentucky Transportation Center Research Report KTC-14-15/SPR460-13-1F, December 2014, https://uknowledge.uky.edu/cgi/viewcontent.cgi?referer=https://www.google.com/&httpsredir=1&article=2486&context=ktc_researchreports at 58.

22. Dug Begley, "Lawmakers Demand Fix for Utility-Related Road Delays," *Houston*

Chronicle, August 12, 2015, http://www.houstonchronicle.com/news/transportation/arti
cle/Lawmakers-demand-fix-for-utility-related-road-6441050.php. See also "Transportation Infrastructure: Impacts of Utility Relocations on Highway and Bridge Projects," 22.

23. "Transportation Infrastructure: Impacts of Utility Relocations on Highway and
Bridge Projects," 23.

24. Michael Stratford, "Endowments Under Fire Again," *Inside Higher Ed,* October
8, 2015, https://www.insidehighered.com/news/2015/10/08/house-republicans-question
-university-endowment-spending-executive-compensation.

25. Kelly Wilz, "Everything You Know about Higher Education is Wrong," *Huffington
Post,* November 2, 2017, https://www.huffingtonpost.com/entry/everything-you-know-
about-higher-education-is-wrong_us_59f09dcce4b0dd88d362d8d7.

26. Monica Davey and Tamar Lewin, "Unions Subdued, Scott Walker turns to Tenure at
Wisconsin Colleges," *New York Times,* June 4, 2015, https://www.nytimes.com/2015/06/05/
us/politics/unions-subdued-scott-walker-turns-to-tenure-at-wisconsin-colleges.html.

27. Hans-Joerg Tiede, "Tenure and the University of Wisconsin System," *AAUP* 102,
no. 3 (May-June 2016), https://www.aaup.org/article/tenure-and-university-wisconsin-
system#.WjkrVFWnFhE.

28. Eric Kelderman, "Wisconsin Lawmakers Take Aim at Tenure and Shared Governance," *Chronicle of Higher Education,* May 31, 2015, https://www.chronicle.com/article/
Wisconsin-Lawmakers-Take-Aim/230545. Tamar Lewin, "Tenure Firmly in Place, but Colleges Grow Wary of Lasting Commitments," *New York Times,* June 6, 2015, https://www.
nytimes.com/2015/06/07/education/tenure-firmly-in-place-but-colleges-grow-wary-of-
lasting-commitments.html.

29. Donald Downs and John Sharpless, "Scott Walker's Latest Crusade Will Hurt Con-
servatives Like Us," *Politico Magazine,* June 23, 2015, http://www.politico.com/magazine/
story/2015/06/scott-walkers-latest-crusade-will-hurt-conservatives-like-us-119341.

30. Thomas Wirth, "The Economics of Peace: World War I and Scott Nearing's Radical
America," *Concept* 27 (2004): 1.

31. "Prof. Brewster Ousted," *New York Times,* June 23, 1915, 6.

32. "Appendix I: 1915 Declaration of Principles on Academic Freedom and Academic
Tenure," *American Association of University Professors,* accessed July 21, 2016, https://www.
aaup.org/NR/rdonlyres/A6520A9D-0A9A-47B3-B550-C006B5B224E7/0/1915Declara
tion.pdf.

33. Frank Donoghue, *The Last Professors: The Corporate University and the Fate of the
Humanities* (New York: Fordham University Press, 2008), 77.

34. Jonathan Cole, "Why Academic Tenure is Essential for Great Universities," *Huffington Post,* November 5, 2010, https://www.huffingtonpost.com/jonathan-r-cole/why-aca
demic-tenure-is-es_b_779440.html.

35. Douglas Belkin, "Colleges, Faced with Funding Cuts, Target Tenure Trims," *Wall
Street Journal,* February 14, 2017, https://www.wsj.com/articles/colleges-faced-with-fund
ing-cuts-target-tenure-trims-1487068202.

36. Sol Gittleman, "Tenure is Disappearing. But It's What Made American Universities
the Best in the World," *Washington Post,* October 29, 2015, https://www.washingtonpost.
com/news/grade-point/wp/2015/10/29/tenure-is-disappearing-but-its-what-made-ameri
can-universities-the-best-in-the-world/?utm_term=.6aba7cc66bf1. Nancy Kendall, "Scott
Walker is Undermining Academic Freedom at the University of Wisconsin," *New Repub-*

lic, June 9, 2015, https://newrepublic.com/article/121999/gov-scott-walker-weakens-ten ure-university-wisconsin. Michael McPherson and Morton O. Schapiro, "Tenure Issues in Higher Education," *Journal of Economic Perspectives* 13, no. 1 (Winter 1999): 85–98.

37. Belkin, "Colleges, Faced with Funding Cuts, Target Tenure Trims."

38. Lewin, "Tenure Firmly in Place, but Colleges Grow Wary of Lasting Commitments."

39. Wilz, "Everything You Know about Higher Education is Wrong."

40. Cole, "Why Academic Tenure is Essential for Great Universities."

41. Donoghue, *The Last Professors.*

42. Robert Markley, "Stop the Presses: A Modest Proposal for Sa(1)vaging Literary Scholarship," *Eighteenth Century: Theory and Interpretation* 29 (1988): 77, as cited in Donoghue, *The Last Professors,* 78.

43. Lewin, "Tenure Firmly in Place, but Colleges Grow Wary of Lasting Commitments."

44. John O. McGinnis and Max Schanzenbach, "College Tenure Has Reached Its Sell-By Date: With Higher Education under Pressure, the Costs and Burdens of This Job Guarantee Need to be Reconsidered," *Wall Street Journal,* August 11, 2015, https://www.wsj.com/articles/college-tenure-has-reached-its-sell-by-date-1439335262.

45. James Wetherbe, "It's Time for Tenure to Lose Tenure," *Harvard Business Review,* March 13, 2013, https://hbr.org/2013/03/its-time-for-tenure-to-lose-te.

46. Caitlin Rosenthal, "Fundamental Freedom or Fringe Benefit?: Rice University and the Administrative History of Tenure, 1935–1963," *AAUP Journal of Academic Freedom* 2 (2011): 3.

47. Stratford, "Endowments Under Fire Again."

48. John Hechinger, "Big-Money Donors Move to Curb Colleges' Discretion to Spend Gifts," *Wall Street Journal,* September 18, 2007, http://www.wsj.com/articles/SB119007667292230616.

49. Hechinger, "Big-Money Donors Move to Curb Colleges' Discretion."

50. David M. Rabban, "A Functional Analysis of 'Individual' and 'Institutional' Academic Freedom under the First Amendment," *Law and Contemporary Problems* 53, no. 3 (1990): 227, 231.

51. Matt Rocheleau, "Federal Lawmakers Query Colleges on Endowments," *Boston Globe,* February 11, 2016, https://www.bostonglobe.com/metro/2016/02/11/lawmakers -ask-wealthy-colleges-for-details-their-billion-dollar-endowments/OsD8TXJ4eyUi4UBcI YiC60/story.html.

52. Victor Fleischer, "Stop Universities from Hoarding Money," *New York Times,* August 19, 2015, http://www.nytimes.com/2015/08/19/opinion/stop-universities-from-hoard ing-money.html?_r=0.

53. "In Elite Schools' Vast Endowments, Malcolm Gladwell Sees 'Obscene' Inequity," August 22, 2015, *Weekend Edition Saturday,* Washington, DC: NPR, http://www.npr.org/2015/08/22/433735934/in-elite-schools-vast-war-chests-malcolm-gladwell-sees-ob scene-inequity.

54. "In Elite Schools' Vast Endowments, Malcolm Gladwell Sees 'Obscene' Inequity."

55. Hechinger, "Big-Money Donors Move to Curb Colleges' Discretion."

56. *Sweezy v. New Hampshire,* 354 U.S. 234, 236, 77 S. Ct. 1203, 1204, 1 L. Ed. 2d 1311 (1957).

57. J. Peter Byrne, "Constitutional Academic Freedom after Grutter: Getting Real about the "Four Freedoms" of a University," *University of Colorado Law Review* 77, no. 4 (2006): 929, 932.

58. *Sweezy v. New Hampshire*, 234.

59. *Sweezy v. New Hampshire*, 262.

60. Byrne, "Constitutional Academic Freedom after Grutter."

61. *Sweezy v. New Hampshire*, 263.

62. "It relied on constitutional academic freedom to decide a major constitutional question that had long been a subject of public and scholarly debate—the constitutionality of racial preferences in higher education admissions. The Court held that the University of Michigan Law School's consideration of race among other factors served a compelling interest in achieving, and was narrowly tailored to achieve, diversity in the student body. The decision provides a new baseline for considering the strength and scope of constitutional academic freedom." Byrne, "Constitutional Academic Freedom after Grutter," 933.

63. Byrne, "Constitutional Academic Freedom after Grutter," 953.

64. "State Tech and Science Index: State Ranking," Milken Institute, accessed March 16, 2016, http://statetechandscience.org/state-ranking.html.

4. Universities as America's Ambassadors-at-Large

1. From remarks delivered at the University of Utah, as recalled by author Michael T. Benson. Chase Peterson was the former president of the University of Utah and vice president of advancement at Harvard under Derek Bok. Peterson is perhaps best remembered, however, for his earlier role at Harvard as dean of admissions, where he aggressively recruited diverse students and hired John S. Harwell, the first African American member of Harvard's admissions staff. Under Peterson's watch as dean, Harvard developed the so-called adjusted system to help foster more diversity; the US Supreme Court cited the system as an example in its pro-affirmative action cases in 1978 and, more recently, in 2005. In a moving on-air eulogy after Peterson's passing, MSNBC's Lawrence O'Donnell divulged that Peterson conducted his own college admissions interview, stating, "Chase Peterson made it the business of the Harvard admissions committee to reach out to minority communities where admission to Harvard was as unheard of as it was in my neighborhood, and he offered a surprisingly warm welcome to highly talented students who otherwise would not have applied." Peterson also admitted Cornel West; West, who went on to become Princeton's first black student to earn a PhD in philosophy, is a noted scholar, activist, and public intellectual. For more on Peterson, see "Lawrence on Dr. Chase Peterson," *The Last Word with Lawrence O'Donnell*, New York: MSNBC, September 15, 2014, http://www.msnbc.com/the-last-word/watch/lawrence-on-dr.-chase-peterson-329552963787, and "Three to Receive HAA Medal for Extraordinary Service," *Harvard Gazette*, April 27, 2006, https://news.harvard.edu/gazette/story/2006/04/three-to-receive-haa-medal-for-extraordinary-service/.

2. Stephanie Saul, "As Flow of Foreign Students Wanes, U.S. Universities Feel the Sting," *New York Times*, January 2, 2018, accessed January 5, 2018, https://www.nytimes.com/2018/01/02/us/international-enrollment-drop.html.

3. Universities have long been recognized as diplomatic assets. For a discussion of how universities, churches, and other institutions act as diplomatic change agents, see Joseph S. Nye Jr., *Soft Power: The Means to Success in World Politics* (New York: PublicAffairs, 2004).

4. George Washington, "Eighth Annual Message to Congress, December 7, 1796." University of Virginia, Miller Center, https://millercenter.org/the-presidency/presidential -speeches/december-7-1796-eighth-annual-message-congress.

5. "Hall of Distinguished Alumni: Sung Chul Yang," University of Kentucky, Alumni Association, accessed August 25, 2015, http://www.ukalumni.net/s/1052/semi-blank-no img.aspx?sid=1052&gid=1&pgid=1497.

6. Sung Chul Yang, "South Korea's Sunshine Policy: Progress and Predicaments," *Fletcher Forum of World Affairs* 25, no. 1 (Winter 2001): 31–41, http://hdl.handle.net/10427/76890.

7. Benjamin Triana, "Cultural Demands of the Host-Nation: International Student Experience and the Public Diplomacy Consequences," *Journal of International Students* 5, no. 4 (2015): 383–394, 387, https://jistudents.files.wordpress.com/2015/05/2015-vol-5-is sue-4-final-book.pdf.

8. Beth McMurtrie, "Opening NAFSA Meeting, Ex-Pentagon Chief Hails Value of Global Programs," *Chronicle of Higher Education,* May 29, 2012, accessed August 24, 2015, http://chronicle.com/article/Opening-Nafsa-Meeting/132035/.

9. "To Alexander Hamilton from George Washington, September 1, 1796," *Founders Online,* National Archives, http://founders.archives.gov/documents/Hamilton/01-20-02 -0199.

10. "To Alexander Hamilton from George Washington, September 1, 1796."

11. Carol Bellamy and Adam Weinberg, "Educational and Cultural Exchanges to Restore America's Image," *Washington Quarterly* 31, no. 3 (2008): 55–68.

12. Bellamy and Weinberg. "Educational and Cultural Exchanges to Restore America's Image," and Barry Fulton, "Geo-Social Mapping of the International Communications Environment or Why Abdul Isn't Listening," *Hague Journal of Diplomacy* 2, no. 3 (2007): 307–315.

13. Gary S. Becker, "What Latin America Owes to the 'Chicago Boys,'" *Hoover Digest,* no. 4 (October 30, 1997), http://www.hoover.org/research/what-latin-america-owes-chica go-boys.

14. Milton Friedman, "Free Markets and the Generals," *Newsweek,* January 25, 1982, 59.

15. Becker, "What Latin America Owes to the 'Chicago Boys.'"

16. Interview with Milton Friedman, "Up for Debate: Reform without Liberty: Chile's Ambiguous Legacy," *Commanding Heights,* Boston: PBS, October 1, 2000, accessed August 25, 2015, http://www.pbs.org/wgbh/commandingheights/shared/minitext/ufd_reformlib erty_full.html.

17. Juan de Onis, "Chile in Crisis: South America's Model Nation Grapples with Graft," *Foreign Affairs,* April 12, 2015, accessed August 25, 2015, https://www.foreignaffairs.com/ articles/chile/2015-04-12/chile-crisis. Javiera Quiroga, "Chile's Economy Grew at 2nd Fastest Pace in 10 Months in January," *Bloomberg,* March 5, 2015, accessed August 25, 2015, http://www.bloomberg.com/news/articles/2015-03-05/chile-s-economy-grew-at-2nd-fast est-pace-in-10-months-in-january.

18. Ben Wolfgang, "Armed with US Education, Many Leaders Take on World," *Washington Times,* August 19, 2012, accessed August 25, 2015, http://www.washingtontimes.com/ news/2012/aug/19/armed-with-us-education-many-leaders-take-on-world/?page=all.

19. "Open Doors 2014: International Students in the United States and Study Abroad by American Students Are at All-Time High," Institute of International Education, November 17, 2014, accessed August 25, 2015, http://www.iie.org/Who-We-Are/News-and-Events/Press-Center/Press-Releases/2014/2014-11-17-Open-Doors-Data.

20. Karin Fischer, "Chinese Students Lead Foreign Surge at US Colleges," *New York Times,* November 30, 2014, accessed August 25, 2015, http://www.nytimes.com/2014/12/01/education/chinese-students-lead-foreign-surge-at-us-colleges.html?_r=0.

21. Moises Naim, "The Case for Giving Iran's Scholar-Diplomats a Chance," *Atlantic,* December 3, 2013, accessed August 25, 2015, http://www.theatlantic.com/international/archive/2013/12/the-case-for-giving-irans-scholar-diplomats-a-chance/282010/.

22. Jay Solomon, "In Iran Nuclear Talks, Two MIT-Trained Physicists Play Key Roles," *Wall Street Journal,* March 17, 2015, accessed August 25, 2015, http://www.wsj.com/articles/in-iran-nuclear-talks-two-mit-trained-physicists-play-key-roles-1426624253.

23. "Open Doors 2014: International Students in the United States and Study Abroad by American Students Are at All-Time High."

24. "The Economic Benefit of International Students," NAFSA, 2014, accessed August 25, 2015, http://www.nafsa.org/_/File/_/eis2014/Kentucky.pdf.

25. "Open Doors Fact Sheet: Kentucky," Institute of International Education, 2014, accessed August 25, 2015, http://www.iie.org/Research-and-Publications/Open-Doors/Data/Fact-Sheets-by-US-State/2014.

26. See Neil G. Ruiz, "The Geography of Foreign Students in U.S. Higher Education: Origins and Destinations," Brookings Institution, August 29, 2014, accessed August 25, 2015, http://www.brookings.edu/research/interactives/2014/geography-of-foreign-students#/M10420.

27. Ruiz, "The Geography of Foreign Students in U.S. Higher Education: Origins and Destinations."

28. Ruiz, "The Geography of Foreign Students in U.S. Higher Education: Origins and Destinations."

29. "Public Opinion Supports International Education," NAFSA, 2012, accessed August 25, 2015, http://www.nafsa.org/_/File/_/2012_edstudentsglobaleconomy.pdf.

30. Susan Pearce, "Enriching American Riches with International Students," *Journal of International Students* 3, no. 1 (2013): i–ii.

31. Stuart Anderson, "International Students Are Vital to U.S. Higher Education," *International Educator* (May/June 2013): 4–8.

32. Stephanie Saul, "Recruiting Students Overseas to Fill Seats, Not to Meet Standards," *New York Times,* April 19, 2016.

33. Saul, "Recruiting Students Overseas to Fill Seats, Not to Meet Standards."

34. Pearce, "Enriching American Riches with International Students."

35. "235. Statement by the President Making Public a Report of the Commission on Higher Education," December 15, 1947, *Harry S. Truman Library and Museum,* http://trumanlibrary.org/publicpapers/index.php?pid=1852.

36. Harry S. Truman "10—Address to the United Nations Conference in San Francisco," April 25, 1945, *American Presidency Project,* Online by John Woolley and Gerhard Peters, accessed August 25, 2015, http://www.presidency.ucsb.edu/ws/index.php?pid=12391.

37. "Fulbright Program History," US Department of State, Bureau of Educational and Cultural Affairs, accessed August 25, 2015, http://eca.state.gov/fulbright/about-fulbright/history.

38. "The Early Years: An Informal History of the Fulbright Program," US Department of State, Bureau of Educational and Cultural Affairs, accessed August 25, 2015, http://eca.state.gov/fulbright/about-fulbright/history/early-years.

39. "The Early Years: An Informal History of the Fulbright Program." See also Francis

A. Young, "Educational Exchanges and the National Interest," *American Council of Learned Societies Newsletter* 20, no. 2 (March 1969): 1–18.

40. "Fulbright Program Impact," Fulbright Association, https://fulbright.org/advoca cy/, cited in Carol Bellamy and Adam Weinberg, "Educational and Cultural Exchanges to Restore America's Image," *Washington Quarterly* 31, no. 3 (2008): 55–68.

41. "Fulbright Program Impact."

42. Elizabeth Redden, "Study Abroad May Lead to Better GPA, Graduation Rates," *USA Today,* July 14, 2010, accessed August 25, 2015, http://www.usatoday.com/news/ed ucation/2010-07-14-IHE-study-abroad-benefits13_ST_N.htm. Heather Barclay Hamir, "Go Abroad and Graduate On-Time: Study Abroad Participation, Degree Completion, and Time-to-Degree" (dissertation, University of Nebraska, 2011), http://digitalcommons.unl. edu/cgi/viewcontent.cgi?article=1065&context=cehsedaddiss.

43. Julia Zimmermann and Franz J. Neyer, "Do We Become a Different Person When Hitting the Road? Personality Development of Sojourners," *Journal of Personality and Social Psychology* 105, no. 3 (2013): 515–530.

44. Ignacio Sabate and Zara Zhang, "Harvard's Global Footprint," *Harvard Crimson,* May 28, 2015, accessed August 25, 2015, http://www.thecrimson.com/article/2015/5/28/ harvard-international-offices-feature/.

45. "Methodology," Academic Rankings of World Universities, ShanghaiRanking Con- sultancy, accessed August 25, 2015, http://www.shanghairanking.com/ARWU-Methodol ogy-2015.html. "Ranking," Academic Rankings of World Universities, ShanghaiRanking Consultancy, accessed August 25, 2015, http://www.shanghairanking.com/ARWU2015. html.

46. "World University Rankings 2014–15," *Times Higher Education,* 2015, accessed Au- gust 25, 2015, https://www.timeshighereducation.co.uk/world-university-rankings/2015/ world-ranking#/sort/0/direction/asc.

47. "U.S. News Global Top 500 Universities," *Washington Post,* accessed August 25, 2015, https://www.washingtonpost.com/apps/g/page/local/us-news-global-top-500-uni versities/1409/.

48. "QS World University Rankings 2014/15," *QS Top Universities,* Quacquarelli Sy- monds, accessed August 25, 2015, http://www.topuniversities.com/university-rankings/ world-university-rankings/2014#sorting=rank+region=+country=+faculty=+stars=false +search.

49. See Derek Bok, *Higher Education in America* (Princeton, NJ: Princeton University Press, 2013).

50. Bok, *Higher Education in America.*

51. "Korean-based INFAC North America Plans $6.5 Million Expansion in Campbells- ville, Kentucky," *AreaDevelopment,* November 15, 2012, accessed August 25, 2015, http:// www.areadevelopment.com/newsItems/11-15-2012/infac-expands-operations-camp bellsville-taylor-county-kentucky8729823.shtml.

52. "South Korean Automotive Supplier INFAC North America to Expand in Camp- bellsville," Think Kentucky, accessed August 25, 2015, https://www.thinkkentucky.com/ newsroom/NewsPage.aspx?x=07312015_INFAC.html.

53. "Report: Kentucky Facilities with Korean Ownership," Think Kentucky, August 3, 2015, accessed August 25, 2015, http://www.thinkkentucky.com/kyedc/kpdf/Korean_ Investment.pdf.

54. "Bourbon and Whiskey Exports Barrel Past $1bn again in 2014," *Guardian,* Febru-

ary 3, 2015, accessed August 25, 2015, http://www.theguardian.com/society/2015/feb/03/kentucky-bourbon-tennessee-whiskey-sales-grow-2014.

55. See Sung Chul Yang, "South Korea's Sunshine Policy: Progress and Predicaments," *Fletcher Forum of World Affairs* 25, no. 1 (Winter 2001), http://hdl.handle.net/10427/76890.

5. A Liberal Education as Part of a Publicly Minded Education

1. "'You've Got to Find What You Love,' Jobs says," commencement address, Stanford University, June 14, 2005, *Stanford News,* http://news.stanford.edu/2005/06/14/jobs-061505/.

2. "'You've Got to Find What You Love,' Jobs says."

3. Steven Johnson, "Marrying Tech and Art," *Wall Street Journal,* August 27, 2011, http://www.wsj.com/articles/SB10001424053111904875404576532342684923826.

4. Walter Isaacson, "The Intersection of the Humanities and the Sciences," *Humanities,* National Endowment for the Humanities, May/June 2014, accessed August 9, 2016, http://www.neh.gov/about/awards/jefferson-lecture/walter-isaacson-lecture.

5. Jonah Lehrer, "Steve Jobs: 'Technology Alone is Not Enough,'" *New Yorker,* October 7, 2011, accessed August 9, 2016, http://www.newyorker.com/news/news-desk/steve-jobs-technology-alone-is-not-enough.

6. Isaacson, "The Intersection of the Humanities and the Sciences."

7. Isaacson, "The Intersection of the Humanities and the Sciences."

8. Amanda Erickson, "A Hillbilly's Plea to the White Working Class," *Washington Post,* August 4, 2016, https://www.washingtonpost.com/opinions/a-hillbillys-plea-to-the-white-working-class/2016/08/04/5c1a7a56-51ca-11e6-b7de-dfe509430c39_story.html?utm_term=.6ad37c48ae88.

9. J. D. Vance, "How the White Working Class Lost Its Patriotism," *Washington Post,* July 25, 2016, accessed August 9, 2016, https://www.washingtonpost.com/posteverything/wp/2016/07/25/how-the-white-working-class-lost-its-patriotism/.

10. J. D. Vance, "The Bad Faith of the White Working Class," *New York Times,* June 25, 2016, http://www.nytimes.com/2016/06/26/opinion/sunday/the-bad-faith-of-the-white-working-class.html?_r=0.

11. 20 U.S.C. § 951 (3–4). See also "The Relevance of Liberal Arts to a Prosperous Democracy: Under Secretary Martha J. Kanter's Remarks at the Annapolis Group Conference," US Department of Education, June 22, 2010, http://www.ed.gov/news/speeches/relevance-liberal-arts-prosperous-democracy-under-secretary-martha-j-kanters-remarks-a.

12. Martha C. Nussbaum, *Not for Profit: Why Democracy Needs the Humanities* (Princeton, NJ: Princeton University Press, 2010); see also Nussbaum, "Cultivating the Imagination," *New York Times,* last updated October 17, 2010, https://www.nytimes.com/roomfordebate/2010/10/17/do-colleges-need-french-departments/cultivating-the-imagination.

13. Daniel H. Pink, *A Whole New Mind: Why Right-Brainers Will Rule the Future* (New York: Penguin, 2006).

14. Adam Frank, "What is the Value of an Education in the Humanities?" 13.7: Cosmos and Culture blog, Washington, DC: NPR, February 2, 2016, http://www.npr.org/sections/13.7/2016/02/02/465239105/what-is-the-value-of-an-education-in-the-humanities.

15. Robert Jensen, "About the School of Art & Visual Studies," University of Kentucky College of Fine Arts, last updated March 5, 2018, http://finearts.uky.edu/savs/about-school-art-visual-studies.

16. James Bruggers, "Kentucky Steps Up Response to Toxic Algae Risks," *Courier-Journal*, updated August 17, 2014, http://www.courier-journal.com/story/tech/science/environment/2014/08/15/checking-drinking-water-risks-toxic-algae/14108539/.

17. "Remarks by the President on Opportunity for All and Skills for America's Workers," White House, Office of the Press Secretary, January 30, 2014, https://www.whitehouse.gov/the-press-office/2014/01/30/remarks-president-opportunity-all-and-skills-americas-workers.

18. Patricia Cohen, "A Rising Call to Promote STEM Education and Cut Liberal Arts Funding," *New York Times*, February 21, 2016, http://www.nytimes.com/2016/02/22/business/a-rising-call-to-promote-stem-education-and-cut-liberal-arts-funding.html?_r=2.

19. Zeynab Day and Brianna White, "Lt. Gov. Says College is a Privilege, Not a Right," *Eastern Progress*, April 7, 2016, http://www.easternprogress.com/2016/04/07/lt-gov-says-college-is-a-privilege-not-a-right/.

20. Alan Rappeport, "Philosophers (and Welders) React to Marco Rubio's Debate Comments," *New York Times*, November 11, 2015, http://www.nytimes.com/politics/first-draft/2015/11/11/philosophers-and-welders-react-to-marco-rubios-debate-comments/?_r=0.

21. Scott Jaschik, "The Shrinking Humanities Major," *Inside Higher Ed*, March 14, 2016, https://www.insidehighered.com/news/2016/03/14/study-shows-87-decline-humanities-bachelors-degrees-2-years. See also "Bachelor's Degrees in the Humanities," Humanities Indicators, American Academy of Arts and Sciences, March 2016, http://humanitiesindicators.org/content/indicatordoc.aspx?i=34.

22. Scott M. Sprenger, "When Humanities Becomes the World," Brigham Young University: Humanities, July 15, 2014, http://humanities.byu.edu/when-humanities-becomes-the-world/.

23. Vinod Khosla, "Is Majoring in Liberal Arts a Mistake for Students?" Medium website, February 10, 2016, https://medium.com/@vkhosla/is-majoring-in-liberal-arts-a-mistake-for-students-fd9d20c8532e#.2pfhp6mwp.

24. Sprenger, "When Humanities Becomes the World."

25. Michael T. Benson, "Liberal Arts Education Essential to Advance in Tech Age," *Lexington Herald-Leader*, February 5, 2016, http://www.kentucky.com/opinion/op-ed/article58708108.html#storylink=cpy.

26. "Entrepreneurship and Social Enterprise (ESE)," Wake Forest University, Wake Forest College, Assessment of Student Learning, http://college.wfu.edu/assessment/program-goals-and-assessments/entrepreneurship-and-social-enterprise-ese/; see also Michael T. Benson, "Point: A Transferable Set of Skills," *Inside Sources*, August 13, 2015, http://www.insidesources.com/point-a-transferable-set-of-skills/.

27. "Humanities+," Brigham Young University, Humanities, accessed July 28, 2016, http://humanities.byu.edu/about-the-college/humanitiesplus/.

28. Emily Friedman, "Mitt Romney Offers Advice on Parental Loans, Majoring in English, and Sticking to the Facts," ABC News blog, New York: ABC News, April 27, 2012, http://abcnewsradioonline.com/politics-news/romney-warns-college-students-dont-believe-everything-you-he.html.

29. Alyson Shontell, "Andreessen: If You Get an English Degree in College, You're Going to End Up Working at a Shoe Store," *Business Insider*, December 12, 2012, http://www.businessinsider.com/sorry-english-majors-but-youre-all-soft-and-destined-to-work-in-a-shoe-store-2012-12.

30. David Brooks, "What Machines Can't Do," *New York Times,* February 3, 2014, http://www.nytimes.com/2014/02/04/opinion/brooks-what-machines-cant-do.html.

31. Erik Brynjolfsson and Andrew McAfee, *The Second Machine Age: Work, Progress, and Prosperity in a Time of Brilliant Technologies* (New York: W.W. Norton & Company, 2014).

32. Frank, "What is the Value of an Education in the Humanities?"

33. *Recruiting Trends 2015–16, 45th ed., Brief 3: Starting Salaries* (East Lansing: Career Services and the Collegiate Employment Research Institute, Michigan State University, 2014–2015), http://www.ceri.msu.edu/wp-content/uploads/2015/10/Recruiting-Trends -Brief-3-Starting-Salaries-10-19-15.pdf.

34. Scott Jaschik, "The Liberal Arts and Careers," *Inside Higher Ed,* April 12, 2012, https://www.insidehighered.com/news/2012/04/12/conference-considers-connection-be tween-liberal-arts-and-careers.

35. Jeffrey T. Steedle and Michael Bradley, *Majors Matter: Differential Performance on a Test of General College Outcomes* (New York: Council for Aid to Education, 2014), http:// cae.org/images/uploads/pdf/Majors_Matter_Differential_Performance_on_a_Test_of_ General_College_Outcomes.pdf.

36. Roger W. Ferguson quoted in *The Heart of the Matter* (Cambridge, MA: American Academy of Arts & Sciences, 2013), 34.

37. J. Bradford Hipps, "To Write Better Code, Read Virginia Woolf," *New York Times,* May 21, 2016, http://www.nytimes.com/2016/05/22/opinion/sunday/to-write-software- read-novels.html?emc=eta1&_r=0.

6. Dynamic Challenges and Solutions in Higher Education

1. Steven J. Spear, *Chasing the Rabbit: How Market Leaders Outdistance the Competition and How Great Companies Can Catch Up and Win* (New York: McGraw Hill, 2009), and Michael A. Cusumano, "Manufacturing Innovation: Lessons from the Japanese Auto Industry," *Sloan Review* (October 15, 1988), http://sloanreview.mit.edu/article/manufactur ing-innovation-lessons-from-the-japanese-auto-industry/.

2. William Mass and Andrew Robertson, "From Textiles to Automobiles: Mechanical and Organizational Innovation in the Toyoda Enterprises, 1895–1933," *Business and Economic History* 25, no. 2 (Winter 1996), http://www.thebhc.org/sites/default/files/beh/ BEHprint/v025n2/p0001-p0038.pdf.

3. Goldie Blumenstyk, *American Higher Education in Crisis?: What Everyone Needs to Know* (New York: Oxford University Press, 2015), 1.

4. Richard Arum and Josipa Roksa, *Academically Adrift: Limited Learning on College Campuses* (Chicago: University of Chicago Press, 2011).

5. As cited in Scott Jaschik, "'Academically Adrift,'" *Inside Higher Ed,* January 18, 2011, https://www.insidehighered.com/news/2011/01/18/study_finds_large_numbers_of_ college_students_don_t_learn_much.

6. Arum and Roksa, *Academically Adrift,* 122.

7. Dan Berrett, "What Should a Major Teach? 'Adrift' Authors Offer Answers," *Chronicle of Higher Education,* June 3, 2016, http://www.chronicle.com/article/What-Should-a- Major-Teach-/236694.

8. Jaschik, "'Academically Adrift.'"

9. David Glenn, "New Book Lays Failure to Learn on Colleges' Doorsteps," *Chronicle of Higher Education,* January 18, 2011, http://www.chronicle.com/article/New-Book-Lays-Failure-to-Learn/125983/.

10. Glenn, "New Book Lays Failure to Learn on Colleges' Doorsteps."

11. Naomi Schaefer Riley, "Should Tenure for College Professors be Abolished?," *Wall Street Journal,* June 24, 2012, http://www.wsj.com/articles/SB10001424052702303610504577418293114042070.

12. Jeffrey F. Milem, Joseph B. Berger, and Eric L. Dey, "Faculty Time Allocation: A Study of Change over Twenty Years," *Journal of Higher Education* 71, no. 4 (July 2000): 472.

13. Hart Research Associates, *Falling Short? College Learning and Career Success: Selected Findings from Online Surveys of Employers and College Students, Conducted on Behalf of the Association of American Colleges & Universities* (Washington, DC: Hart Research Associates, 2015), https://www.aacu.org/sites/default/files/files/LEAP/2015employerstudentsurvey.pdf, and Scott Jaschik, "Well-Prepared in Their Own Eyes," *Inside Higher Ed,* January 20, 2015, https://www.insidehighered.com/news/2015/01/20/study-finds-big-gaps-between-student-and-employer-perceptions.

14. Alina Tugend, "What it Takes to Make New College Graduates Employable," *New York Times,* June 28, 2013, http://www.nytimes.com/2013/06/29/your-money/a-quest-to-make-college-graduates-employable.html.

15. "2016 Workforce-Skills Preparedness Report," *PayScale,* May 2016, http://www.payscale.com/data-packages/job-skills.

16. Arum and Roksa, *Academically Adrift,* 145.

17. Kevin Carey, "'Academically Adrift': The News Gets Worse and Worse," *Chronicle of Higher Education,* February 12, 2012, http://www.chronicle.com/article/Academically-Adrift-The/130743/.

18. Carey, "'Academically Adrift': The News Gets Worse and Worse."

19. Arum and Roksa, *Academically Adrift,* 144.

20. Arum and Roksa, *Academically Adrift,* 145.

21. Heidi Shierholz, Alyssa Davis, and Will Kimball, "The Class of 2014: The Weak Economy is Idling Too Many Young Graduates," *Economic Policy Institute,* May 1, 2014, http://www.epi.org/publication/class-of-2014/.

22. Shierholz, Davis, and Kimball, "The Class of 2014." See also Sandy Baum, Jennifer Ma, and Kathleen Payea, "Education Pays 2013: The Benefits of Higher Education for Individuals and Society," College Board, 2013, and "Annual Social and Economic Supplement to the Current Population Survey," Washington, DC: US Census Bureau, US Department of Commerce.

23. Benjamin Ginsberg, "Administrators Ate My Tuition," *Washington Monthly,* September/October 2011, http://washingtonmonthly.com/magazine/septoct-2011/administrators-ate-my-tuition/.

24. Ming Zhang and Sharon Schmidtz, "Benchmark Report: Ratio of Faculty to Administrators," Western Washington University, Office of Institutional Research, January 2013, https://www.wwu.edu/provost/communication/documents/BenchmarkReport_FacultytoAdminRatio.pdf, 3.

25. Jon Marcus, "New Analysis Shows Problematic Boom in Higher Ed Administrators," *New England Center for Investigative Reporting,* February 6, 2014, http://www.huffingtonpost.com/2014/02/06/higher-ed-administrators-growth_n_4738584.html.

26. Laura Pappano, "How the University of Alabama Became a National Player," *New York Times,* November 3, 2016, http://www.nytimes.com/2016/11/06/education/edlife/survival-strategies-for-public-universities.html?rref=collection%2Ftimestopic%2FTuition.

27. Thomas G. Mortenson, "State Funding: A Race to the Bottom," *American Council on Education,* Winter 2012, http://www.acenet.edu/the-presidency/columns-and-features/Pages/state-funding-a-race-to-the-bottom.aspx.

28. Pappano, "How the University of Alabama Became a National Player."

29. Pappano, "How the University of Alabama Became a National Player."

30. Spear, *Chasing the Rabbit.*

31. Steven J. Spear and H. Kent Bowen, "Decoding the DNA of the Toyota Production System," *Harvard Business Review* (September/October 1999), https://hbr.org/1999/09/decoding-the-dna-of-the-toyota-production-system.

32. Martin Fackler, "The 'Toyota Way' is Translated for a New Generation of Foreign Managers," *New York Times,* February 15, 2007, http://www.nytimes.com/2007/02/15/business/worldbusiness/15toyota.html?adxnnl=1&adxnnlx=1428581964–6eXrj+mRCoaU4jkVusb0LA.

33. Jon Gertner, "From 0 to 60 to World Dominion," *New York Times Magazine,* February 18, 2007, http://www.nytimes.com/2007/02/18/magazine/18Toyota.t.html?pagewanted=all&_r=0.

34. David Magee, *How Toyota Became #1: Leadership Lessons from the World's Greatest Car Company* (New York: Penguin, 2007).

35. Yuri Kageyama, "Toyota's Profit Slides 18.5 Percent on Tsunami Disaster's Effects," *Huffington Post,* November 8, 2011, http://www.huffingtonpost.com/2011/11/08/toyotas-profit-tsunami_n_1081532.html?; Craig Trudell and Yuki Hagiwara, "Toyota Fends off VW to Stay Biggest Carmaker a Third Year," *Bloomberg,* January 20, 2015, http://www.bloomberg.com/news/articles/2015-01-20/toyota-fends-off-volkswagen-to-stay-top-automaker-for-third-year.

36. Janet Napolitano, "Higher Education Isn't in Crisis," *Washington Post,* March 12, 2015, https://www.washingtonpost.com/opinions/higher-education-isnt-in-crisis/2015/03/12/f92b777e-bba2-11e4-bdfa-b8e8f594e6ee_story.html.

37. Thomas St. Myer, "Ball State, Ex-Classmates Share David Letterman Tales," *Star Press,* April 6, 2014, http://www.indystar.com/story/entertainment/movies/2014/04/05/ball-state-ex-classmates-share-david-letterman-tales/7358109/.

38. Goldie Blumenstyk, "Blowing Off Class? We Know," *New York Times,* December 2, 2014, http://www.nytimes.com/2014/12/03/opinion/blowing-off-class-we-know.html.

39. Blumenstyk, "Blowing Off Class? We Know."

40. Blumenstyk, "Blowing Off Class? We Know."

41. Janel Davi, "Georgia State University Tracks Data to Boost Graduation Rates," *Atlanta Journal-Constitution,* February 4, 2015, http://www.centerdigitaled.com/higher-ed/Georgia-State-Tracks-Data-to-Boost-Graduation-Rates.html.

42. Daphne Koller, Andrew Ng, and Zhenghao Chen, "Retention and Intention in Massive Open Online Courses: In Depth," *Educause Review,* June 3, 2013, http://www.educause.edu/ero/article/retention-and-intention-massive-open-online-courses-depth-0.

43. "Ricks College to Become Brigham Young University-Idaho," BYU Idaho, June 21, 2000, http://www2.byui.edu/transitionannouncement.htm.

44. *Online Learning,* BYU Idaho, accessed April 14, 2018, https://byupathway.lds.org/.

45. "What is PathwayConnect?," Pathway: In Partnership with BYU Idaho, accessed May 17, 2015, https://pathway.lds.org/Main/Information.

46. "How Pathway Works," Pathway: In Partnership with BYU Idaho, accessed May 17, 2015, https://pathway.lds.org/Main/Standard.

47. "Cost," Pathway: In Partnership with BYU Idaho, accessed May 17, 2015, https://pathway.lds.org/Main/Cost.

48. Howard M. Collett, "Pathway Provides Opportunity for a Brighter Future," *Church News,* May 6, 2013, https://www.lds.org/church/news/pathway-provides-opportunity-for-a-brighter-future?lang=eng.

49. Anya Kamenetz, "Southern New Hampshire University: For Relentlessly Reinventing Higher Ed, Online and Off," *Fast Company,* February 7, 2012, http://www.fastcompany.com/3017340/most-innovative-companies-2012/12southern-new-hampshire-university.

50. Gabriel Kahn, "The Amazon of Higher Education: How Tiny, Struggling Southern New Hampshire University Has Become a Behemoth," *Slate,* January 2, 2014, http://www.slate.com/articles/life/education/2014/01/southern_new_hampshire_university_how_paul_leblanc_s_tiny_school_has_become.html.

51. St. Myer, "Ball State, Ex-Classmates Share David Letterman Tales."

52. Mike Cullity, "Innovation U," *Extra Mile* (Spring 2012): 16, April 6, 2014, https://academicarchive.snhu.edu/bitstream/handle/10474/2298/extramilespring2012.pdf?sequence=1&isAllowed=y.

7. Higher Education at Work for the Commonwealth

1. In this chapter we draw on previously published writing from the authors, especially Michael Benson, "The Meaning and Purpose of the University," *Huffington Post,* February 2, 2017, https://www.huffingtonpost.com/michael-benson/the-meaning-and-purpose-o_b_14608092.html.

2. "Gilman's Inaugural Address," Johns Hopkins University, accessed January 11, 2017, https://www.jhu.edu/about/history/gilman-address/.

3. "Gilman's Inaugural Address."

4. "Enrollment & Demographics," University of Kentucky Institutional Research and Advanced Analytics, Fact Book, accessed December 20, 2017, https://www.uky.edu/iraa/enrollment-demographics.

5. Glenn Farley, "Boeing: Airlines Will Need 617,000 Pilots, 814,000 Attendants," *USA Today,* August 1, 2016, http://www.usatoday.com/story/travel/flights/todayinthesky/2016/08/01/boeing-projects-hiring-demand-for-global-airlines/87579998/.

6. "Enrollment," Eastern Kentucky University Office of Institutional Research, Fact Book, accessed December 20, 2017, http://ir.eku.edu/factbook-2016-2017.

7. "No-Tuition Promise," Berea College, accessed January 11, 2017, https://www.berea.edu/.

8. Michael Benson, "A Graduation Unlike Any Other," *Huffington Post,* May 7, 2016, accessed January 11, 2017, http://www.huffingtonpost.com/michael-benson/a-graduation-unlike-any-o_b_7224548.html.

9. The seven liberal arts colleges that make up the "Work Colleges Consortium" are Berea, Alice Lloyd, Ecclesia, Sterling, Blackburn, Warren Wilson, and the College of the Ozarks. Work Colleges Consortium, http://www.workcolleges.org/.

10. "Appalachian Leaders College Scholarship," Alice Lloyd College, Leadership U, http://www.alc.edu/admissions/financial-aid/appalachian-leaders-college-scholarship/.

11. "Student Work Program," Alice Lloyd College, Leadership U, http://www.alc.edu/admissions/financial-aid/student-work-program/.

12. Adrienne Raphel, "The Work-College Revival," *New Yorker,* April 12, 2015, http://www.newyorker.com/business/currency/the-work-college-revival.

13. "Student Work Program," Alice Lloyd College, Leadership U.

14. Raphel, "The Work-College Revival."

15. Alice B. Lloyd, "Inside Appalachian Work Colleges—Where Students Labor to Learn," *Weekly Standard,* November 14, 2016, http://www.weeklystandard.com/inside-appalachian-work-colleges-where-students-labor-to-learn/article/2005281.

16. Raphel, "The Work-College Revival."

17. Scott Carlson, "The Future of American Colleges May Lie, Literally, in Students' Hands," *Chronicle of Higher Education,* February 5, 2012, http://www.chronicle.com/article/Tools-for-Living/130615/.

18. "History," Berea College, Labor Program Office, https://www.berea.edu/labor-program-office/history/. Raphel, "The Work-College Revival."

19. "Workplace Expectations," Berea College, Human Resources, https://www.berea.edu/human-resources/workplace-expectations/.

20. "Student Work Handbook," Alice Lloyd College, http://www.alc.edu/wp-content/uploads/2012/06/Student-Work-Program-Handbook.pdf.

21. Raphel, "The Work-College Revival."

22. "About Human Resources," Berea College, Human Resources, accessed January 11, 2017, https://www.berea.edu/human-resources/.

23. "History," Berea College, Labor Program Office.

24. "History," Berea College, Labor Program Office.

25. Mark Green, "Learning to Work at Berea College," *Lane Report,* May 9, 2013, http://www.lanereport.com/21136/2013/05/learning-to-work-at-berea-college/.

26. "Welcome," Berea College, Labor Program Office, https://www.berea.edu/labor-program-office/.

27. "Goals and Purposes," Berea College, Labor Program Office, https://www.berea.edu/labor-program-office/goals/.

28. "How We Give Tuition Promise Scholarships," Berea College, Give to Berea, https://www.berea.edu/give/a-worthy-investment/how-we-give-tuition-promise-scholarships/.

29. "National Report Shows Berea College Has Lowest Tuition and Fees in the Nation," Berea College, News, https://www.berea.edu/news/national-report-shows-berea-college-has-lowest-tuition-and-fees-in-the-nation/.

30. Jeff Amburgey, "Berea College Written Statement," to the Committee on Ways and Means Hearing, September 13, 2016, Berea College, Office of Financial Affairs, https://waysandmeans.house.gov/wp-content/uploads/2016/09/20160913-OS-Testimony-Amburgey.pdf.

31. Tamar Lewin, "With No Frills or Tuition, a College Draws Notice," *New York Times,* July 21, 2008, http://www.nytimes.com/2008/07/21/education/21endowments.html.

32. Mark Twain, *The Innocents Abroad* (Hartford, CT, 1869).

33. "Study Abroad at Centre College," Centre College, Flyer, http://www.centre.edu/wp-content/uploads/2016/02/study_abroad_flyer.pdf.

34. "Open Doors Report," Institute of International Education, http://www.iie.org/Who-We-Are/News-and-Events/Press-Center/Press-Releases/2016/2016-11-14-Open-Doors-Data#.WJY98FMrLIU.

35. Stephanie Saul, "As Flow of Foreign Students Wanes, U.S. Universities Feel the Sting," *New York Times*, January 2, 2018, https://www.nytimes.com/2018/01/02/us/international-enrollment-drop.html.

36. "Open Doors Report," Institute of International Education.

37. "Open Doors Report," Institute of International Education.

38. "Centre College Again Ranked #1 in the Nation for Study Abroad," Centre College, News, November 17, 2014, https://www.centre.edu/centre-college-again-ranked-1-in-the-nation-for-study-abroad/.

39. "Centre is Your Passport: Studying Abroad Easier Than Ever," Centre College, News, August 29, 2013, https://www.centre.edu/centre-is-your-passport-studying-abroad-easier-than-ever/.

40. Michael Strysick, "Centre Ranked No. 1 in the Nation for Study Abroad," *Centrepiece* 54:2.

41. "Centre is Your Passport: Studying Abroad Easier Than Ever," Centre College, News, https://www.centre.edu/centre-is-your-passport-studying-abroad-easier-than-ever/.

42. "#3 in the Nation for Study Abroad," Centre College, Study Abroad, https://www.centre.edu/about-6/study-abroad/.

43. Milton Reigelman, "Globalizing the Curriculum," *Centrepiece* 54:2.

44. Leigh Ivey Cocanougher, "International Internships," *Centrepiece* 54:2.

45. Strysick, "Centre Ranked No. 1 in the Nation for Study Abroad."

46. Milton Reigelman, "Internationalizing the Campus through Internationalizing the Faculty," *Centrepiece* 54:2.

47. Reigelman, "Globalizing the Curriculum."

48. "Research Investigates Another 'Kentucky Ugly,'" University of Kentucky, College of Medicine, Center of Excellence in Rural Health, accessed January 11, 2017, https://ruralhealth.med.uky.edu/news/research-investigates-another-kentucky-ugly.

49. Laura Ungar, "What Ails Appalachia Ails the Nation," *USA Today*, August 7, 2014, http://www.usatoday.com/story/news/nation/2014/08/07/appalachia-health-cdc-frieden-disease/13643547/.

50. Ungar, "What Ails Appalachia Ails the Nation."

51. Dean Praetorius, "2010 Census: Poorest Counties in America," *Huffington Post*, December 21, 2010, http://www.huffingtonpost.com/2010/12/21/2010-census-the-poorest-c_n_799526.html.

52. "Appalachian Translational Research Network (ATRN)," University of Kentucky, Center for Clinical and Translational Science, http://www.ccts.uky.edu/ccts/appalachian-translational-research-network-atrn#aboutus.

53. Frank Browning, "Diabetes in Appalachia: 'Just Give Me a Pill,'" *Salon TV*, August 8, 2012, http://www.salon.com/2012/08/08/diabetes_in_appalachia_just_give_me_a_pill/.

54. "Appalachian Translational Research Network (ATRN)."

55. Bruce Behringer and Gilbert H. Friedell, "Appalachia: Where Place Matters in Health," *Preventing Chronic Disease* 3, no. 4 (October 2006), https://www.cdc.gov/pcd/issues/2006/oct/06_0067.htm#appalachian.

56. Center for Excellence in Rural Health, Ky. Rev. Stat. § 164.937.

57. Center for Excellence in Rural Health, Ky. Rev. Stat. § 164.937.

58. "About Kentucky Homeplace," University of Kentucky, College of Medicine, Center of Excellence in Rural Health, http://ruralhealth.med.uky.edu/about-kentucky-homeplace.

59. "About Kentucky Homeplace."

60. F. J. Feltner, G. E. Ely, E. T. Whitler, D. Gross, and M. Dignan, "Effectiveness of Community Health Workers in Providing Outreach and Education for Colorectal Cancer Screening in Appalachian Kentucky," *Social Work in Health Care* 51, no. 5 (2012): 430–440.

61. "About Kentucky Homeplace."

62. Frances Feltner, Sydney Thompson, William Baker, and Melissa Slone, "Community Health Workers Improving Diabetes Outcomes in a Rural Appalachian Population," *Social Work in Health Care* 56, no. 2 (2017): 115–123.

63. Feltner, Ely, Whitler, Gross, and Dignan, "Effectiveness of Community Health Workers in Providing Outreach and Education for Colorectal Cancer Screening in Appalachian Kentucky."

64. David McCullough, *The Wright Brothers* (New York: Simon & Schuster, 2015).

65. Jelisa Castrodale, "How Many Flights Cross the USA in a Day?," *USA Today*, April 27, 2016, http://www.usatoday.com/story/travel/roadwarriorvoices/2016/04/27/us-flight-activity/83572030/.

66. Bureau of Transportation Statistics: 201 US-Based Airline Traffic Data. https://www.bts.gov/newsroom/2017-annual-and-december-us-airline-traffic-data.

67. Kate Murphy, "Plenty of Passengers, but Where are the Pilots?," *New York Times*, April 16, 2016, accessed January 11, 2017, https://www.nytimes.com/2016/04/17/opinion/sunday/plenty-of-passengers-but-where-are-the-pilots.html?_r=0.

68. "About EKU Aviation: History," Eastern Kentucky University, Aviation, http://aviation.eku.edu/about-eku-aviation.

69. "EKU Aviation—Moving Forward with Innovation," Eastern Kentucky University, Aviation, slideshow, http://slideplayer.com/slide/5694171/.

70. "About EKU Aviation: History."

71. Ricki Barker, "Time to Fly: Top Hawk Aviation Program to Touch Down at EKU in February," *Richmond Register*, December 27, 2016, http://www.richmondregister.com/news/time-to-fly-top-hawk-aviation-program-to-touch-down/article_53c36f5a-cc97-11e6-8caf-db1117f368bc.html.

72. "EKU Aviation—Moving Forward with Innovation."

73. Eastern Kentucky University Aviation, http://www.eku.edu/news/aviation-program-teams-expressjet-airlines-provide-majors-career-pathway.

74. Barker, "KY: Top Hawk Aviation Program to Touch Down"; Barker, "Time to Fly."

75. "Top Hawk 2017," Textron Aviation, http://txtav.com/en/top-hawk.

76. "Path to Career in Aviation," *New Horizons*, 48 (April 2015): 2.

Conclusion

1. Thomas G. Mortenson, "State Funding: A Race to the Bottom," *American Council on Education*, Budget and Appropriations (Winter 2012), accessed December 21, 2016, http://www.acenet.edu/the-presidency/columns-and-features/Pages/state-funding-a-race-to-the-bottom.aspx.

2. Michael Ash and Shantel Palacio, "Economic Impact of Investment in Public Higher Education in Massachusetts: Short-Run Employment Stimulus, Long-Run Public Re-

turns," PHENOM Update, April 2012, accessed December 27, 2016, http://phenomonline. org/wp-content/uploads/2015/10/AT-2012-Ash-Report-5-4.pdf.

3. Paul Krugman, "The Uneducated American," *New York Times,* October 8, 2009, http://www.nytimes.com/2009/10/09/opinion/09krugman.html.

4. We are drawing from previously published writings on this topic, specifically Michael Benson, "Two Public Policies That Transformed Our Nation," *Huffington Post,* June 21, 2014, updated August 21, 2014, https://www.huffingtonpost.com/michael-benson/two-public-policies-that-_b_5516662.html.

5. Benson, "Two Public Policies That Transformed Our Nation."

6. Franklin D. Roosevelt, "Message to Congress on the Education of War Veterans," October 27, 1943. Online by Gerhard Peters and John T. Woolley, *The American Presidency Project,* http://www.presidency.ucsb.edu/ws/?pid=16333.

7. William G. Bowen and Michael S. McPherson, *Lesson Plan: An Agenda for Change in American Higher Education* (Princeton, NJ: Princeton University Press, 2016), 3–4.

8. Here we draw from previously published writings on this topic, specifically Michael Benson, "The March for Science and American Higher Education," *Huffington Post,* April 25   2017,   https://www.huffingtonpost.com/entry/the-march-for-science-and-american -higher-education_us_58fe717ae4b0f420ad99caf7; "Public Research Universities: Changes in State Funding," 2, American Academy of Arts and Sciences, accessed December 22, 2016, https://www.amacad.org/multimedia/pdfs/publications/researchpapersmonographs/ PublicResearchUniv_ChangesInStateFunding.pdf.

9. "Public Research Universities: Changes in State Funding," 4.

10. Jonathan R. Cole, "Can American Research Universities Remain the Best in the World?," paragraph 2, *Chronicle of Higher Education,* January 3, 2010, https://www.chroni cle.com/article/the-clouded-future-of-american/63353.

11. Bob Davis, "There's an Antidote to America's Long Economic Malaise: College Towns," *Wall Street Journal,* December 12, 2012, accessed December 21, 2016, https:// www.wsj.com/articles/theres-an-antidote-to-americas-long-economic-malaise-college-towns-1481558522.

12. Pew Charitable Trusts, *Federal and State Funding of Higher Education: A Changing Landscape* (Washington, DC: Pew Charitable Trusts, 2015), 3, fig. 2.

13. Council for Aid to Education, *Voluntary Support of Higher Education, 2016* (New York: Council for Aid to Education, 2017), 2, fig. 1.

14. National Center for Education Statistics, "Fast Facts: Tuition Costs of Colleges and Universities," https://nces.ed.gov/fastfacts/display.asp?id=76.

15. National Center for Education Statistics, "The Condition of Education: Undergraduate Enrollment," accessed December 21, 2016, http://nces.ed.gov/programs/coe/in dicator_cha.asp.

16. Bowen and McPherson, *Lesson Plan: An Agenda for Change in American Higher Education,* 3.

17. Speech to House of Commons (June 15, 1874), https://api.parliament.uk/historic -hansard/commons/1874/jun/15/motion-for-a-select-committee.

Index